CALLED
TO BE A
CHAMPION

THE ULTIMATE BIBLE-BASED PLAYBOOK FOR YOUNG ATHLETES

CYRUS ELLISON

101 "1-MIN" DEVOTIONS

SPORTS DEVOTIONALS TO BUILD DISCIPLINE, MENTAL TOUGHNESS, AND A GROWTH MINDSET

FROM:

TO:

DATE:

NOTE:

Disclaimer and Legal Notice

PRAISE

champions God's way. Our teens are quoting verses during warmups now. That is real discipleship in motion. It is short, relevant, and rooted in truth. Every parent, coach, and youth leader should have a stack of these ready to hand out.

Linda R., Bible Study Group Leader

Our Sunday sports moms' Bible study chose Called to Be a Champion as our spring devotional, and it became our favorite season yet. Each chapter turns everyday athletic struggles into spiritual insight. We saw ourselves in the players' discipline, our kids' ups and downs in competition, and our own need for quiet time before chaos. The reflections are beautifully written and grounded in Scripture, with practical "Practice" steps that keep the lessons real. We laughed, prayed, and even started doing short gratitude drills before the school run. This book does not just inspire; it equips. It reminds us that being a champion is not about trophies but about training the soul to trust God through pressure, victory, and everything in between

TABLE OF CONTENTS

CHAPTER 3 - TRUE IDENTITY

CHAPTER 4 – WHEN YOU'RE IN A SLUMP

CHAPTER 5 – THE REAL GAME

CHAPTER 6 – STRONGER TOGETHER

00

INTRO: CALLED TO BE A CHAMPION

The gym is still dark.

One light flickers over the floor.

You breathe out and watch it rise in the cold air. Shoes tied. Head down. Heart awake.

This is where it begins.

Champions are not built under bright lights. They are built when no one is watching. When it is too early, too quiet, or too hard. That is why this book exists. Steph Curry doesn't wait for cameras. He gets up before the world does and talks to God while the coffee is still brewing.

Giannis Antetokounmpo stays on the court after everyone leaves, feet sore, heart steady, eyes locked on one more drill.

Simone Biles breathes slow, blocks out the noise, and balances like her peace depends on it.

Tom Brady once threw footballs at a taped X on a wall until he could hit it perfectly in his sleep.

Michael Phelps practiced with flooded goggles and still won gold because he trusted his count and his calm.

Every story in this book shows what happens when faith meets discipline. When you choose focus over fear. When you believe that God trains you through the grind.

This is not a book to skim. It is a book to live.

Each page gives you one quick devotion: a verse to reset your mind, a story to fire you up, a prayer to center your heart, and a small action you can take right away.

» You will learn how to win the morning, starting your day like Jesus did, quiet and grounded before the world starts yelling.

» You will run for the prize, chasing purpose instead of likes or stats.

» You will practice in private so your public moments feel peaceful and ready.

» You will train when no one sees, knowing God is cheering in the silence.

» You will take one more rep when everything inside says stop.

» You will build mindset before muscle so you win longterm.

» You will finish what you start when the world tells you to quit.

» You will learn how to play free, not fearful, because faith beats fear.

Some days you will crush it. Some days you will forget. That is okay.

If you miss a day, you did not fail. You just made room to improve. Pick it up again. Each restart is another rep for your character. Champions fall and get back up. That is how they grow.

God already sees potential in you that is bigger than any scoreboard. You were created to be strong, not just in your sport, but in your spirit. This book is here to help you find that strength and build it one minute at a time.

So grab your sneakers. Grab your Bible. Take a breath.

» You are not just practicing drills. You are training your heart.

» You are not just chasing wins. You are chasing purpose.

» You are **CALLED** to be a **CHAMPION**.

HOW TO USE THIS BOOK

1. One a day.

Each devotion takes about a minute. Read it before first period, before practice, or right after a game. Small steps become big results.

2. Read. Reflect. Pray. Practice.

It's a simple flow. Read the verse. Picture the story. Pray the short prayer. Then do the one small action. Repeat tomorrow.

3. Miss a day? You're fine.

Everyone slips. Just restart. Champions are not perfect, they are persistent.

4. Bring your team in.

Read one together before warmups. Talk about it after practice. Share a line in your group chat. Faith grows stronger in community.

5. Track your growth.

Keep a small notebook or notes app. Write one thing that hit you. Over time, you will see how much you have changed.

Now take a deep breath.

Feel the energy building.

The lights are coming on. The clock is ticking.

You are about to see how faith can sharpen focus, calm nerves, and make every rep, drill, and game feel different.

Turn the page. Your story as a champion starts now.

CHAPTER 01 - DISCIPLINE THAT LASTS

01

WIN THE MORNING

"Very early in the morning, while it was still dark, Jesus went to a solitary place and prayed." Mark 1:35

The arena still glittered with confetti, tiny stars caught in shoelaces. Steph Curry slipped into a quiet tunnel, trophy under one arm, jersey damp with joy. He sat on a plastic crate, closed his eyes, and remembered the kitchen at 5 a.m. A dim lamp. Steam curling from a mug. Sneakers waiting like friendly dogs by the door. He whispered thanks before the sun colored the blinds.

Those simple minutes became a lighthouse for crazy days. Jesus met His Father in the dark and walked out with light. You can too. Before alarms scream and group chats explode, give God the first word. Picture your day opening like a gym door. Hear the bounce of a ball in a silent gym. Feel peace settle your shoulders like a warm hoodie. Start with gratitude, a verse, a breath. By homeroom, you carry calm. By practice, your mind is clear, your heart steady, your joy real.

Prayer:

Lord, thank You for today. Meet me first, settle my mind, focus my heart, and lead my steps with You.

Practice:

Pray before phone. Thank God, breathe slowly, smile, and name one top priority today first.

02
RUN FOR THE PRIZE

"Run in such a way as to get the prize." 1 Corinthians 9:24

Golden sunset on the track. Usain Bolt laced his spikes while crickets tuned like a tiny orchestra. No crowd. Just the soft thud of strides and a coach's measured clap. He lifted his eyes past the finish line, picturing more than medals. He saw discipline shaping character, patience in the blocks, humility in interviews, kindness with fans.

Temporary trophies sleep in glass cases. Eternal rewards change who you become. Paul wrote about running to truly win. That begins when you choose purpose over impulse. Homework before gaming. Sprints after mistakes. Scripture before scrolling. Each choice is a step toward a prize that outlasts the podium. Imagine God smiling at your effort, not because you are perfect, but because you are faithful. Tie your shoes with intention. Read the verse. Then run your drills as worship. The clock can measure speed, but only God can measure why. When your why is eternal, your legs find another gear and your heart finds peace.

Prayer:

Lord, focus me on You. Aim my choices toward Your prize. Shape habits that honor eternity in my sport today.

Practice:

Read the verse before practice. Choose one phrase to steer effort, attitude, and pace today.

03
PRACTICE IN PRIVATE

"Whoever is faithful with very little will also be faithful with much." Luke 16:10

Night breath fogged in small clouds as Tom Brady stayed on a lonely field. Cones glowed under cheap stadium lights. He threw at a taped X on a net until the ball kissed the target like a habit. No music. No hype. Just rhythm. The secret is this. Repetition writes truth into your muscles. Faithfulness in small things becomes confidence in big moments. God sees driveway dribbles, basement footwork, and quiet playbook study at a kitchen table. When the stands roar, your body remembers the secret song you taught it. Your nerves listen to the calm you built in silence. Think of your room as a lab where excellence grows roots. Ten clean minutes today can turn into ten fearless seconds on game day. Do not chase applause. Chase accuracy. Close your door, whisper a prayer, and practice until right feels normal. Then, when the lights blare, you will simply play what you practiced, peaceful and ready.

Prayer:

Father, see my effort. Grow small secret work into steady confidence, strong habits, and calm under lights for Your glory.

Practice:

Do ten solo push ups. Count slow, keep form, breathe rhythmically, and thank God sincerely.

04
TRAIN WHEN NO ONE SEES

"Pray to your Father who is unseen. Then your Father who sees what is done in secret will reward you." Matthew 6:6

Batting cage. Humming lights. Mookie Betts tracked seams like tiny planets spinning toward him. Crack. Net rustle. Reset. He worked the boring corners, not just the heroic swings. In that quiet, he whispered quick prayers and chased one pure sound. God was there, unseen, cheering the hidden grind. When you shut the door on noise and choose one drill, heaven notices. Rewards arrive as quick reads, soft hands, and a heart that does not panic. Build a secret place. Maybe it is your garage, the driveway, or the far hoop at the park. Bring honesty. Bring attention. Bring a notebook. Over weeks, roots thicken underneath the surface. Later, under pressure, you do not chase approval. You simply breathe and play what you have practiced. That is freedom, the kind that lasts longer than cheers. Train in secret, and your public moments will carry holy calm.

Prayer:

Father, bless my secret work. Meet me in quiet places and grow unseen fruit that lasts through patient daily faith.

Practice:

Do one extra drill alone. Silence notifications, set a timer, give full attention the whole time.

05

ONE MORE REP

"No discipline seems pleasant at the time, but painful. Later it produces a harvest of righteousness and peace." Hebrews 12:11

Empty gym. Echoing bounce. Michael Jordan's hands were raw, but the ball kept returning like a promise. He missed. Adjusted. Hit. Missed again. Stayed. One more rep is a small door that opens to a wide field. Pain knocks, but wisdom invites it to teach. God uses controlled discomfort to grow courage and patience. Picture your muscles writing letters to your future self. Dear Tomorrow, we learned to push without fear. When practice burns, breathe in a verse and breathe out doubt. Hard is not the enemy. Sloppy is. Push with form, listen to your body, rest smart, then add the clean extra. Weeks from now, the moment that once scared you will feel familiar. Peace will stand where panic used to live. You will smile, remembering a quiet gym and a brave extra rep that changed everything inside you.

Prayer:

Lord, give me grit. Protect my body, guide my form, and grow courage through every challenge I face this week.

Practice:

Add one extra rep today. Slow, perfect form, full breath, and finish strong with confidence.

06

MINDSET BEFORE MUSCLE

"Be transformed by the renewing of your mind." Romans 12:2

Still water. Early echo. Michael Phelps sat on the starting block, eyes closed, building a race inside his head. He felt the cold, saw the wall, heard the hush right before the horn. He pictured clean entries, sharp turns, steady breathing. Then his body simply followed the script his mind rehearsed. God renews minds so bodies can perform with peace. Replace fear movies with truth movies. Before practice, imagine the good. See clean footwork. Hear your coach's cue. Feel a steady heart beating like a drum for God. Whisper a verse to set your pace. When your thoughts align with truth, pressure shrinks and skill flows. Preparation becomes worship. Performance becomes a gift back to Him. Train your brain first, and your muscles will listen like loyal teammates.

Prayer:

Jesus, renew my mind. Replace fear with truth, rush with peace, and help my body follow faith today.

Practice:

Thirty seconds of visualization. Close eyes, breathe slowly, picture perfect reps, then go perform calmly.

07
FINISH WHAT YOU START

"Do not grow weary in doing good, for at the proper time we will reap if we do not give up." Galatians 6:9

Gym clock blinked late. Giannis Antetokounmpo faced a stubborn ladder drill that kept tripping his feet. Sweat dotted the floor like rain on pavement. He wanted to quit. He chose to finish. That choice planted a pattern. Weeks later, in a wild fourth quarter, his feet moved without panic, as if guided by rails. Finishing small tasks trained a finish in big moments. God promises a harvest for those who keep going. You feel it in chores, homework, recovery exercises, and free throws. Each completion is a seed. You may not see sprouts today, but roots are growing. Start one task. Complete it. Then smile. You are becoming a finisher. Your teammates will trust you. Your heart will trust you. When the game asks for courage at the end, you will already know how to close.

Prayer:

Lord, keep me finishing. Give me patient energy to complete good work even when I feel tired.

Practice:

Complete one delayed task today. Small or big, finish fully, and thank God for strength.

A QUICK BLESSING

Your feedback is a true blessing!

If this book has encouraged you or helped you feel less alone, would you leave a quick review?

Even one sentence makes a huge difference and takes just a minute. As a small author, your feedback not only lifts my heart... it also helps other children of God find the support and hope they need.

Thank you for being part of this journey!

Scan this QR code with your phone to go to the review page

Or

Go to your orders, find the book and click

"Write a product review"

Thank you <3

You can use this page for any notes you want to take so far, or reflect any changes you have noticed to your routines or feelings.

08
YOUR WHY BEATS FEELINGS

"Whatever you do, work at it with all your heart, as working for the Lord."
Colossians 3:23

Night film room glow. Patrick Mahomes leaned forward, pausing plays with quiet curiosity. Friends were out, but purpose kept him there. His why was bigger than feelings. He plays to honor God, love his family, and serve teammates. Your feelings rise and fall like waves. Your why is an anchor. When you remember who you serve, training turns from chore to calling. Write your reason where your eyes land daily. When practice starts, repeat it like a password. Purpose turns average drills into worship. It turns nerves into focus. You stop asking, do I feel like it, and start saying, this is who I am. Work for the Lord with all your heart, and watch confidence grow from the inside out.

Prayer:

Father, remind me why. Fix my heart on You so I serve with joy beyond moods today.

Practice:

Write my why on paper. Keep it in bag, read before practice, speak it aloud.

09
DISCIPLINE OVER MOOD

"Everyone who competes goes into strict training." 1 Corinthians 9:25

Alarm blinks 4:30. City quiet. Kobe Bryant tied his shoes and let the morning air wake his lungs. Some days felt heavy. He showed up anyway. He stacked quiet sessions into quiet strength until discipline became a friend. The Bible calls it strict training. Schedules can guard your calling when moods wobble. Set times. Keep them. Use habits like train tracks that carry you even when motivation is low. God meets you in steady effort and grows maturity. Others drift between feelings. You stack small wins. By game time, you walk in with a soft smile, knowing the work is banked. That calm humbles pressure. That rhythm builds greatness one early choice at a time.

Prayer:

God, make me steady. Help me train with purpose when feelings wobble, and let consistency grow joy.

Practice:

Track habits one week. Sleep, prayer, practice, study. Check boxes daily, then review progress.

10
BUILD SYSTEMS NOT HYPE

"The plans of the diligent lead to profit, as surely as haste leads to poverty." Proverbs 21:5

Manny Pacquiao, boxing legend and follower of Jesus, ties his shoes before sunrise in General Santos City. Street quiet. Air cool. No cameras. He runs the same route, prays the same prayer, and logs the same rounds. Reporters love knockouts, but Manny loves notebooks. Before a title fight, he showed one page already mapped: roadwork, stretch, spar, Bible reading, nap, recovery. Feelings are loud on fight week, he said, but feelings fade. Systems stay. Proverbs 21:5 taught him careful plans turn small choices into big results. At school and practice, this looks like packing your bag at night, setting alarms, prepping meals, and scheduling reps. You stop waiting to feel ready. You follow your map when friends are late, when classes pile up, when nerves rise. Pray, Order my steps. Routine does not shrink you. It stabilizes you, so you can grow when pressure hits. Build your system tonight and let tomorrow follow like clockwork. Enjoy the calm, repeat daily.

Prayer:

Lord, guide my planning and protect my focus. I choose steady steps. Order my steps today, tomorrow, always, now. Amen.

Practice:

Tonight plan tomorrow: wake, school, training, meals, homework, Scripture, recovery, lights out. Follow it closely.

11
SELF CONTROL IS POWER

"I strike a blow to my body and make it my slave." 1 Corinthians 9:27

Russell Wilson treats small choices like game winners. He guards sleep like treasure, screens like a gate, and words like seeds. That is not boring. That is power. Self control is steering the car instead of riding in the trunk. The verse shows an athlete who leads desires to serve a higher mission. You can train the same way. Choose water over soda. Homework before scrolling. Encouragement over gossip. Ask God to help you lead your body, not follow every craving. Over time, you will notice sharper focus, kinder speech, and faster recovery. Doors open for athletes who can tell themselves no, then yes to what matters most.

Prayer:

Jesus, master my self. Teach me to lead my body and choices so they honor You daily.

Practice:

Skip one temptation today. Food, screen, or gossip. Say no, breathe, and thank God.

12

SWEAT IS WORSHIP

"Offer your bodies as a living sacrifice, holy and pleasing to God." Romans 12:1

Chalk dust sparkled in the light as Simone Biles stood at the beam, breathing slow. She could feel the room listening. She knew every routine could be an offering. Not to judges first, but to God. Your body is a gift. Training can become worship when you bring effort with gratitude. Stretch with care like you are tuning an instrument. Lift with focus like you are building a cathedral. Treat teammates with love. This turns practice into something holy. You are not just getting stronger. You are telling God thank You with each honest rep. When you finish, the sweat on your forehead is like an amen.

Prayer:

Lord, use my effort. Receive my training as worship and make my attitude kind, grateful, and joyful.

Practice:

Pray before workout. Invite God into warm ups, drills, and cool down. Say thank You.

13

CONSISTENCY WINS

"A sluggard's appetite is never filled, but the desires of the diligent are fully satisfied." (Proverbs 13:4)

Tyson Fury, heavyweight boxing champion, slides on his gloves in a quiet gym before sunrise. Rope snaps the floor, bag thumps, sweat dots the canvas. No crowd, only footsteps and a stopwatch. He logs rounds, sleep, water, and verses in a beat up notebook. Some days feel flat, lungs heavy, jokes quiet. He shows up anyway. By fight night, consistency has stacked like bricks. Confidence comes from receipts.

Proverbs 13:4 says desire is not enough. The diligent are satisfied because they do the small things daily. That works for you too. Ten serves after dinner. Thirty minutes of homework. One page of Scripture. Text a teammate, then show up again tomorrow. Keep the chain and the chain will keep you. When emotions wobble, your routine holds you steady. Pray, Make me consistent, then follow your plan with joy. Gold belts are shiny, but quiet habits are the real crown that no one can take. Repeat tomorrow, then repeat again. Always.

Prayer:

Father build steady habits in me. When I feel lazy, strengthen will. Make me consistent, faithful, joyful, and focused. Amen.

Practice:

Open your tracker, mark today, restart if needed, one rep, one prayer, keep going, daily.

14

NEVER CUT CORNERS

"Whoever walks in integrity walks securely." Proverbs 10:9

Practice ended. Music faded. Aaron Judge jogged back to the cage. Coach had called it, but he stayed to fix one sloppy swing path. No shortcut. That choice built trust with others and with himself. Integrity in training gives security in games. When you cut corners, you plant doubt that shows up later as shaky hands. When you finish drills correctly, you plant confidence that shows up as calm. God smiles on honest work. Walk straight today. Choose accuracy over speed and truth over convenience. Your future self will thank you. Precision right now becomes courage later when everything is loud.

Prayer:

Lord, keep me honest. Help me love accuracy and truth in every drill, word, and choice.

Practice:

Perfect one drill slowly. Hit every detail. Do not rush. End only when form is clean.

15
SHOW UP ANYWAY

"Diligent hands will rule." Proverbs 12:24

Some mornings LeBron James felt heavy. He showed up anyway. He started with a stretch, a sip of water, and a simple prayer. Soon his body warmed and rhythm returned like a song he knew by heart. He learned that effort before emotion unlocks momentum. Feelings are real, but they are not the boss. God honors steady hands. When you begin, energy often follows. Start small. Lace shoes. Touch the line. Do the first drill early. By the time your mood notices, you are already moving. Captains are made one early yes at a time, until teams start to trust your steady pace.

Prayer:

Father, help me show up. Give me starter courage and grow strength as I keep going today.

Practice:

Do first drill early. Set a timer, begin immediately, and let momentum carry you today.

CHAPTER 2 – MIND OVER PRESSURE

16

CALM UNDER PRESSURE

"Do not be anxious about anything... and the peace of God... will guard your hearts and your minds in Christ Jesus." — Philippians 4:6–7

Night air buzzing like bees. Student section shaking the rails. Tim Tebow stood at the line, sweat rolling, chest thumping like a drum. He gripped the laces and felt the leather cool his palm. One breath. The world slowed, like someone turned the volume knob down. He whispered, "Calm my heart." A surrender. The play before was chaos. Now he pictured it simple. Snap. Step. Read. Checkdown. He took what was there, moved the chains, and the stadium blur turned into focus. Pressure visits you too. Free throws while your crush watches. Last lap when legs burn like fire. Your brain screams hurry, and your hands get jumpy. Prayer flips the script. Talk to God, then act. Peace guards your chest like a shield. You still hustle, but panic stops. Your eyes widen. Options appear. The game feels winnable again. Calm is muscle you train by choosing it early, not only in emergencies. Today, practice the pause. Breathe slow, invite God in, then play with poise. Like a Champ!

Prayer:

Lord, when pressure comes, calm my heart. Trade my panic for Your peace. Guard my mind and guide my decisions.

Practice:

Inhale four, hold two, exhale four. Repeat twice. Whisper, Calm my heart, then run your next play confidently.

17

PLAY FREE, NOT FEARFUL

"For God gave us a spirit not of fear but of power and love and self-control."
— 2 Timothy 1:7

Cold start. Shots rimmed out. Steph Curry glanced at his wrist where tiny ink read Faith > Fear. He smiled like a kid at recess. The crowd buzzed hot, but inside he felt backyard quiet. He bounced the ball to a playful rhythm, shoulders loose, eyes bright. One buttery release. Net sang. Another. The game opened like a window letting fresh air in. Freedom did not mean he never missed. It meant he remembered Who gave the gift and why he plays. Fear grabs your throat in school gyms too. You grip the ball like it might escape. Your moves get stiff. Faith opens your hands. Power from God steadies your core. Love reminds you it is bigger than your stats. Self-control keeps your shot smooth. Play for God's smile, not for everyone's approval. If you miss, you learn. If you score, you serve your team with joy. Either way, you are free. Decide before tip: faith first. Then bring that bright, creative game the court was built to see.

Prayer:

Father, free me from fear. Fill me with Your power, love, and clear mind. Help me play loose, joyful, and brave.

Practice:

Write Faith > Fear on tape or shoe. See it, breathe, smile, then attack the next play with freedom.

18
PRESSURE IS A PRIVILEGE

"From everyone who has been given much, much will be demanded." — Luke 12:48

Night sky glittered with phone lights. Coco Gauff started tight, forehand flying long. She walked to the towel box and whispered, "Thank You for moments like this." Gratitude felt like flipping a heavy switch. Shoulders dropped. Feet found their bounce. She swung brave, lifting the ball deep, painting lines. The crowd's roar turned from a threat into wind in her sails. Pressure stopped feeling like punishment. It felt like trust.You feel it too. Coach points to you for the final serve. Friends chant your name. Your stomach flips like a roller coaster. Try Coco's secret: reframe. Say, "I am trusted. I am ready." God often hands responsibility to the prepared. Gratitude turns shaking hands into steady ones. Your brain clears. You stop playing not to lose and start playing to honor the gift. Pressure can sharpen you like a whetstone if you thank God in it. When the moment swells, smile. Breathe. Receive it as assignment, not attack. Compete with a light heart.

Prayer:

Lord, thank You for big moments. Grow my capacity, steady my nerves, clear my vision, and help me honor You today.

Practice:

When stress spikes, inhale slowly and say, Pressure means trust. Exhale. Step in and swing boldly at the next chance.

19

CONFIDENCE IS A CHOICE

"Be strong and courageous… for the Lord your God is with you wherever you go." — Joshua 1:9

Pocket shrinking. Criticism swirling like gnats. Jalen Hurts knelt, pressed fingers into the turf, and felt the cool earth ground him. He stood tall and chose courage. Not loud swagger. Quiet steel. He locked eyes with his huddle. Play call. Snap. Footwork crisp, throws decisive, chains moving. He did not wait to feel confident. He acted from the truth that God was with him. Your confidence will wobble on quiz days and game days. Do not wait for magic feelings. Choose your source. If God is with you, you can step forward. Decide your tone before the whistle. Strong effort. Humble heart. Clear leadership. Confidence grows each time you pick it again. The more you practice it, the more your body remembers. Your feet plant. Your voice steadies. Your game opens. Let your calling set your courage. Work hard in quiet places. Trust God in loud ones. Then play like you belong, because you do.

Prayer:

God, remind me You are with me. Make me bold in effort, humble in heart, and steady in every hard moment.

Practice:

Write three recent wins. Read them out loud. Thank God for each. Carry the list into practice confidently.

20

WHEN CROWD IS LOUD

"Be still, and know that I am God." — Psalm 46:10

Away gym trembling. Drums pounding like thunder. Giannis Antetokounmpo stood at the stripe and shut his eyes for a heartbeat. He felt the ball's pebble grip, heard his own breath, and let the noise fade to a hum. One simple cue in his mind. Bend. Lift. Follow through. The net barely moved. He did not fight the crowd. He found stillness inside it.

You cannot mute a packed gym or a bus full of teammates. But you can train a quiet center. Stillness is not doing nothing. It is choosing the One who holds everything. Loosen your jaw. Drop your shoulders. Focus on one clean thought. Let the chants become background music while you move with calm purpose. God is bigger than their volume and closer than your heartbeat. When you know that, your hands get soft and your choices get smart. Practice daily stillness so it shows up on noisy nights. Quiet becomes your secret advantage.

Prayer:

Jesus, be my stillness in noise. Quiet my racing thoughts, steady my hands, and help me hear Your gentle guidance.

Practice:

Close eyes for thirty seconds. Breathe softly. Repeat, Still my soul. Open, choose one cue, then act with calm.

21
FOCUS OVER FEAR

"You keep him in perfect peace whose mind is stayed on you, because he trusts in you." — Isaiah 26:3

Warm water wrapped Michael Phelps like a blanket. Before finals, he sank beneath the surface and swam the race in his mind. Strokes counted. Turns sharp. Finish fierce. In one final, his goggles flooded. Darkness. No panic. He trusted his stroke count and the plan he pictured. Touch. Gold. Peace rode on focus.

Fear scatters your attention like spilled marbles. Focus gathers it into a straight line. Fix your thoughts on God's steady character. Build a clear plan. See it with detail. Name one simple cue. When chaos arrives, ride the plan you practiced. You do not need perfect conditions in a loud stadium or windy field. You need trust and a target. Keep your mind stayed, and your body will follow like a train on tracks.Peace is not empty. It is anchored. Choose your anchor before the whistle, and storms will not own you.

Prayer:

Lord, keep my mind stayed on You. Trade my worry for focus. Give me steady peace and sharp decisions today.

Practice:

Before the start, visualize the whole play. See pace, timing, finish. Whisper, Guard my mind. Execute your first cue.

22

BREATHE AND BELIEVE

"Then the Lord God formed the man… and breathed into his nostrils the breath of life." — Genesis 2:7

Pocket messy. Crowd hot. Joe Burrow reset with a slow inhale, like a wave rolling in, then a steady exhale, like the tide sliding out. The huddle watched his chest settle. Their eyes settled too. Next snap, he hit the seam, first down, rhythm restored. Breath became leadership without a speech.

God's breath began your story. Your breath can restore your focus. When anxiety climbs your ribs, own your oxygen. In through the nose, calm and cool. Out through the mouth, long and light. Pray, "Fill me with life," as the air moves. Heart rate drops. Tension leaks out of your shoulders. Vision widens. Your timing returns. You do not need to shout over nerves. You need to breathe beneath them. Train it when you tie your shoes, not only when alarms blare. A calm breath is a quiet superpower.

Prayer:

Breath of God, fill me with life. Settle my chest, sharpen my mind, and center my spirit for this moment.

Practice:

Use four-count box breathing. In four, hold four, out four, hold four. Whisper, Fill me with life.

23
WHEN YOU MISS THE SHOT

"Though the righteous fall seven times, they rise again." — Proverbs 24:16

Buzzer close. LeBron James missed a dagger three. The arena gasped. He did not pose or pout. He sprinted back, cut off a drive, ripped the rebound, and kicked ahead for the go-ahead bucket. Failure became fuel in seconds. He treats misses like messages, not names.

You will miss. Maybe with your friends watching, maybe with a phone recording. Let the sting teach without sticking to your identity. Review the footwork. Note the angle. Adjust the release. Then choose courage again. In Christ you are called righteous, not flawless. Rising is your pattern. The more you rise, the faster you rise. Resilience grows like a muscle. Write the lesson, not the label. Forgive quickly, learn quickly, move forward with a clear head and bright eyes. Champions bounce, not break.

Prayer:

Father, lift me again after misses. Give me courage to take the next shot with wisdom, patience, grit, and joy.

Practice:

Write one sentence lesson from the miss. Keep it. Release the guilt. Take the next shot confidently.

24
TRUST GOD'S TIMING

"He has made everything beautiful in its time." — Ecclesiastes 3:11

Third string. Scout team. Brock Purdy threw routes to starters who barely knew his name. He watched, learned, and kept sharpening tiny details. Footwork clean. Eyes calm. Heart steady. When his number was called, the moment felt like a door he had already walked through in practice a thousand times. Beauty arrived right on schedule.

Waiting rooms are classrooms in God's world. Delays feel like closed doors, but often they are slow ovens where strength bakes. God is not late. He is layering skills and character so success does not crush you. Use the quiet days. Add one tool. Strengthen one weakness. Serve your team even if no one claps. Pray for patience, not shortcuts. When the door opens, you will fit the room. Your job is readiness and trust. God's job is timing. Stay faithful, and one day people will say overnight. You will know the truth.

Prayer:

God, guide my steps when doors pause. Teach me patience. Shape my character. Prepare my skills. Align opportunity with Your glory.

Practice:

Write one blessing from waiting. Thank God. Train one small skill today with cheerful, steady faithfulness.

25

SILENCE THE CRITIC

"There is therefore now no condemnation for those who are in Christ Jesus."
— Romans 8:1

Halftime headache. Trevor Lawrence sat on the bench, eyes closed, while the inner critic shouted like a broken alarm. He opened his Bible app, whispered the verse, and pictured placing his guilt at Jesus' feet. Shoulders softened. Jaw unclenched. He returned to the huddle light and led a patient comeback. Grace makes space for skill.

Your loudest critic might be living rent free in your head. Catch the thought. Ask, Is it true, helpful, from God? If not, evict it. Replace it with Scripture. Speak grace over your game. Correction matters. Condemnation kills joy. Jesus already carried your shame. Compete from acceptance, not for acceptance. A clear conscience clears your mechanics. Let truth be your soundtrack. Let grace be your ground. Then go play brave, smart, and free.

Prayer:

Lord, silence condemning voices. Let Your no condemnation promise anchor me. Replace lies with grace, purpose, courage, and confidence.

Practice:

Catch one harsh thought. Replace with Scripture truth. Say it aloud three times with calm conviction.

26

COMPOSURE IS CONTAGIOUS

"The one who has knowledge uses words with restraint." — Proverbs 17:27

Timeout. Down five. Kawhi Leonard's eyes were quiet lakes. No flapping arms. No frantic speech. He took one slow breath, tapped a teammate's chest, and called a simple action. The bench settled like dust after wind. Next possession, good screen, clean pass, tough finish. The room borrowed his calm and played better.

You set the climate. Panic spreads like smoke. Peace spreads like sunlight. When things wobble, lower your voice. Move with purpose. Use clear, short words. Model belief with your face and your feet. People mirror what you carry. If you carry peace, they will find theirs faster. Leadership is not always loud. It is steady, clear, and kind. Be the thermostat, not the thermometer. Set the temperature of trust, and watch your team breathe again.

Prayer:

Jesus, use my calm to lead. Help my eyes, words, and pace spread steady confidence to teammates in tough moments.

Practice:

Model slow breathing and simple calls. Huddle teammates. Say, Use my peace. Guide the next play with poise.

27
GAME-DAY PRAYER

"Some trust in chariots and some in horses, but we trust in the name of the Lord our God." — Psalm 20:7

The arena hummed like a giant fridge, ice mist floating under bright lights. Mike Fisher, veteran NHL center and former Predators captain, checked his skates and glanced at the room. He had routines like everyone else: tape, stretch, sip. But playoffs bring noise that routines cannot quiet. Fisher, a committed Christian, husband, and team-first leader in pro hockey, stood and said, "Circle up." Helmets touched. He led a short, honest prayer: "Lord, be my confidence." Not superstition. Surrender.

When the puck dropped, chaos rushed him. Hits thumped. Sticks snapped. He repeated the line between breaths. Calm rose. Vision cleared. He won faceoffs, encouraged rookies, and played free. The prayer did not promise goals. It planted trust where fear wanted roots. Peace spread along the bench like warmth in winter. You can lead that moment at your game. One clear sentence, spoken with faith, can reset the whole room. Invite teammates. Ask God to carry the weight you keep grabbing. Then compete hard, smiling, because confidence lives in Him today, always.

Prayer:

Jesus, be my confidence today. Quiet fear, steady focus, guide my words, my feet, my heart, and my team. Amen.

Practice:

Before warmups, gather teammates and lead a brief prayer: "Lord, be our confidence today." together

28

GOD'S PEACE OVER PRESSURE

"Peace I leave with you; my peace I give to you… Let not your hearts be troubled." — John 14:27

Pocket exploding like popcorn. Patrick Mahomes slid right, reset his feet, and found still water inside the storm. That calm did not start at the snap. It started in quiet times, learning to receive Jesus' peace like a gift you never run out of. With that peace, he saw windows others missed and turned chaos into creation.

Pressure wants your steering wheel. Hand it to Christ instead. His peace is not thin ice. It is bedrock. Breathe, remember the promise, then run the play. Let peace lead your cadence, your eyes, and your voice. Pressure may still pound on the door, but it does not get the keys. With Christ's peace, you can execute in traffic and bring calm to your huddle. Make peace your pregame habit. Hide the verse in your heart. When trouble knocks, the promise answers.

Prayer:

Prince of Peace, steady me in chaos. Let Your calm lead my eyes, words, timing, and choices through competition.

Practice:

Memorize John 14:27. Repeat it on the sideline when nerves rise. Breathe once, then execute the next read.

29
CLUTCH FAITH

"All things are possible for one who believes." — Mark 9:23

Tie game. Clock hissing down. Stephen Curry caught the pass and shrunk the world to one small circle of light at the rim. He breathed once, whispered the verse in his heart, and trusted his hours of lonely reps. The ball lifted like it knew where to go. Sometimes the net sings. Sometimes it rattles out. His belief stays steady either way.

Your clutch will come. Last serve. Final kick. Corner three. Do not look for magic. Look for trust. Say the verse. See the target. Stack your feet the way you trained. Let your body do its job while your heart rests in God. If it drops, praise Him. If it misses, praise Him and be ready for the next. Clutch faith is practiced trust meeting prepared skill, not superstition.

Play bold, not wild. Believe big, work smart, and let God hold the outcome.

Prayer:

Lord, I believe. Help my unbelief. Meet me in clutch moments. Give me courage, clarity, and a faithful heart.

Practice:

Before your next big attempt, whisper the verse. Breathe once. Trust your work. Release smooth. Run back ready.

CHAPTER 3 - TRUE IDENTITY

30
MORE THAN A STAT LINE

"I praise You because I am fearfully and wonderfully made." (Psalm 139:14)

Lincoln Financial Field glittered like a city of stars as Carson Wentz broke the huddle. Breath steamed in the cool night. The ball snapped, linemen thundered, and he zipped a laser between two defenders. Touchdown. The place shook like a drum. Hours later the noise was gone. Tape still clung to his wrists. The locker room hummed softly, like a seashell at your ear. Carson stared at the stat sheet glowing on his phone. Big numbers. Big praise. But his chest felt strangely empty, like a trophy case with one light off. He whispered Psalm 139. If God formed every thread of him, then his worth did not report to the scoreboard.

He replayed God's gifts the cameras missed. The grit to rehab when no one clapped. The voice to lift a teammate drowning in doubt. The calm to own a mistake. He smiled. Pressure slid off like sweat. Identity first. Performance second. You are built by God with care. Your value does not wobble when your stats do. Play free. Play with joy. Let the God who made you define you.

Prayer:

Thank You for me. You made me wonderfully. Teach me to play from worth, not for it, with peace today.

Practice:

List three God given traits. Thank Him for each before practice or study.

31
ALREADY APPROVED

"Nothing can separate us from the love of God in Christ Jesus." (Romans 8:38–39)

The lights cooled and the chatter swirled as Trevor Lawrence walked through the tunnel after a rough night. Sweat dried cold on his neck. Reporters hovered like moths around a porch lamp. Trevor slipped into a quiet hallway and breathed. Romans 8 rose like a strong song. No loss could cut him from God's love. The next morning the film room glowed blue. Click. Missed read. Click. Late throw. He paused the screen and prayed under his breath. Already loved. Already held. That approval felt like a heavy anchor in windy water. He wrote fixes on a card, then crossed the locker room to encourage a receiver who had dropped a sure score. Loved people love people. You will have nights that sting. Remember the seatbelt of Romans 8. Buckle it before practice. It lets you look truth in the eyes without panic. It frees you to lead with a quiet smile, because your heart is not begging for likes. It is resting in Love.

Prayer:

Let me rest in Your love. Teach me to learn from losses, lead with peace, and walk secure today.

Practice:

After your next loss, thank God for three lessons gained. Share one lesson with a teammate kindly.

32

BE YOU, NOT THE HYPE

"Do not think of yourself more highly than you ought, but rather with sober judgment." (Romans 12:3)

Chase Center trembled when Klay Thompson's first three splashed. The net whispered. The crowd jumped like a wave. He grinned, felt the joy, then later sat at his kitchen table with a sandwich and a notebook. The house was quiet, the kind of quiet that tells the truth. He wrote two lines. Be honest. Be grateful. Hype can puff you up like a balloon or pop you and leave rubber on the floor. Truth keeps shape. Romans 12:3 became Klay's mirror. Not too big. Not too small. He listed gifts and growth. Smooth release. Tough defense. Patient leadership. Better footwork. Deeper trust. He thanked God for both the made shots and the misses that taught him. You live in hype winds too. Clips, comments, whispers in hallways. Let God be your mirror. Confidence without ego. Humility without hiding. When you carry the real you into practice, everything feels lighter. You stop acting. You start living.

Prayer:

Keep me humble and honest. Clear out hype and fear. Help me serve my team with steady confidence.

Practice:

Write a real me list. One strength, one weakness, one action to help your team today.

33
CHARACTER OVER CLOUT

"People look at the outward appearance, but the Lord looks at the heart." (1 Samuel 16:7)

Maya Moore knew the rush of a packed arena. Banners breathed from rafters. Cameras trailed her every step. Then she did something stunning. She stepped away to fight for justice for a man in prison. The lights dimmed. The applause paused. But heaven leaned in. First Samuel 16 says God reads hearts like open books. Maya chose the paragraph that matters most. Integrity over image. Love over likes. She visited courtrooms, wrote letters, and prayed late when the world slept. That story glows brighter than any title, because it shows who she is when the scoreboard is silent. Your stage may be a gym with squeaky floors or a bus seat after practice. Character grows in hidden places. Tell the truth. Keep your word. Pick up trash no one saw you drop. Text a quiet teammate and check in. Clout fades like chalk in rain. Character roots like an oak and shelters others.

Prayer:

Grow my heart. Make me honest when it costs. Give me strength to choose right over easy every day.

Practice:

Find one teammate's unnoticed effort. Give a specific, sincere compliment. Thank them for lifting the group.

34

IDENTITY BEFORE PERFORMANCE

"Whatever you do, work at it with all your heart, as working for the Lord." (Colossians 3:23)

Boos rumbled like distant thunder, and the rink felt heavy. Ivan Provorov, sturdy NHL defenseman for Philadelphia, tightened his gloves and breathed slow. He is known for dependable two-way play, convictions, and a quiet Christian faith that guides choices beyond headlines. Pressure swirled. Opinions flew. One truth steadied him: Audience of One. He whispered verse while lining up at the blue line. Not for applause. Not for clicks. Not even for coaches first. For the Lord. That target purifies effort. He blocked a shot, pain buzzing through his skate, and chased the rebound. He made the next right play. Identity before performance. Gift before game. When you play for God's approval, you stop chasing claps and start chasing excellence with peace. Mistakes turn into lessons, not labels. You hustle when stands are quiet, and you share credit when cameras arrive. Ask God to search motives before practice. Write the phrase where you will see it. Then skate, shoot, and smile, because you already belong. Freedom fuels focus.

Prayer:

Father, purify my motives. I want Your approval. Clean my heart, correct pride, and make my effort worship today. Amen.

Practice:

Write "Audience of One" on gear. Read it before drills, and games.

35

CONFIDENCE FROM THE CROSS

"I can do all things through Christ who strengthens me." (Philippians 4:13)

The warmup music thumped as Steph Curry laced his shoes. A verse was inked small near the heel, like a secret map. He spun the ball, smiled, and shot as if joy lived in his wrists. Not because he never felt pressure. Because he knew who carried him through it. Philippians 4:13 is not a magic spell. It is a steady bridge over any situation. Hot streaks need humility. Cold nights need courage. Finals pressure needs peace. Steph still drills the tiny things. Foot angle. Balance. Follow through. But his deepest steady is Jesus, who met him on good nights and sat with him after bad ones. Let the cross be your confidence. If God gave His best there, He will not leave you under bright lights here. Breathe deeper. Trust your work. Trust Him more. Take the next right shot. Live the next right play. Joy will meet you.

Prayer:

My strength is You. Fill me with courage from Christ. Help me play bold, calm, and joyful today.

Practice:

Write Philippians 4:13 on tape, socks, or a notebook. Read it before your first rep.

36
BODY AS GIFT

"Your body is a temple of the Holy Spirit." (1 Corinthians 6:19)

The stadium track looked like a red river under the sun. Allyson Felix crouched in the blocks, a mother now, a fighter still. She exhaled a thank You that felt like warm light in her chest. She stopped seeing her body as a machine she must whip and started seeing it as a gift she must steward.

Training shifted. Fuel became worship. Sleep became obedience. Stretching became prayer with movement. She noticed the miracle of ankles that roll and recover, lungs that sing, a heart that keeps time. Gratitude softened frustration and sharpened discipline. You may wish for a different height, faster genetics, or a flashier frame. Tell your mirror the truth. God formed you for purpose. When you honor your body, you build a life that can hold greatness. Set a bedtime. Drink water. Learn mobility. Celebrate slow, steady gains. That is not boring. That is holy.

Prayer:

Help me honor You with my body. Teach me to rest, fuel, train, and recover with thankful discipline.

Practice:

Stretch slowly tonight. Thank God out loud for three body parts and what they let you do.

37
MIRROR VS MESSAGE

"The Lord is my light and my salvation. Whom shall I fear." (Psalm 27:1)

Between routines, Gabby Douglas could hear everything. The cheers. The nitpicks. The quick takes that sting like tiny bees. In the mirror she saw her own face, tired and brave. She whispered Psalm 27. God is my light. The room felt brighter, like someone opened a window.

When Gabby chose God's voice, her posture changed. Chin up. Shoulders back. She moved with the looseness that comes when lies have no chair. The beam looked less like a test and more like a stage for trust. You face mirrors too. Photos, comments, thoughts that point at your flaws with sharp fingers. Let God's light be your reflection. He says you are loved, strong, and not alone. Tape that message to your heart. Let it set your face before you step out. Darkness cannot boss you around when the Light stands beside you.

Prayer:

You are my light. Chase away lies and fear. Help me see myself the way You do today.

Practice:

Write a short Scripture affirmation on a sticky note. Place it where you get ready.

38

COMPARISON KILLS CALLING

"What is that to you. You must follow Me." (John 21:22)

Christian Pulisic sat on the bus scrolling headlines. More minutes for someone else. Bigger contract for another. His stomach knotted. Then he remembered Jesus talking to Peter in John 21. Do not look sideways. Follow Me. Christian put the phone away and stared out at the night, streetlights sliding past like slow stars. Peace slipped back in. Comparison steals your breath. It turns practice into a courtroom and friends into rivals. God is not grading you against the teammate with fancy cleats. He is shaping you in your lane. Runner's eyes forward. Celebrate others, then return to your assignment. Study film. Nail the next drill. Learn the small details no one applauds. Trust God to open the doors that have your name on them. When your eyes stop wandering, your feet start flying. Joy returns. Growth speeds up.

Prayer:

Focus me on Jesus. Turn my head from comparison. Help me follow You with effort, joy, and clarity.

Practice:

Mute one account that triggers envy. Replace it with Scripture, training tips, or quiet prayer.

39

GOD DOES NOT BENCH YOU

"Do not fear, for I am with you. I will uphold you." (Isaiah 41:10)

Some nights Jayson Tatum watched the game from the sideline more than the floor. The bench felt like a lonely island. Cameras drifted elsewhere. He tightened his laces and prayed Isaiah 41. God holds me. That promise felt like a warm hand around a cold one.

He decided the bench would be his new battleground. He tracked plays, called out screens, and met teammates with clear eyes and quick encouragement. When his number came, he was ready like a sprinter in the blocks. Coaches noticed. Trust grew. Your role might shrink for a while. God's presence will not. Staying ready is holy work. Learn the game. Support loudly. Find the detail no one is handling and handle it. Even if your minutes stay small, heaven measures differently. Faithful is big there.

Prayer:

Hold me steady when my role changes. Keep me ready, joyful, and helpful to every teammate today.

Practice:

If you are on the bench, pick one teammate. Offer specific, helpful encouragement on their role.

40

PLAY FROM GRATITUDE

"Give thanks in all circumstances." (1 Thessalonians 5:18)

After surgery, Cooper Kupp walked slow laps around the field. Tape tugged. Muscles ached. He counted gifts like treasures in grass. Breath in lungs. Sun on face. Trainers who cared. Friends who prayed. Gratitude did not ignore pain. It changed the color of the day. Back in games, he kept counting. The chalk dust on his gloves. The rhythm of cleats. The beauty of a route clicking on time. Thankfulness made pressure lighter and focus sharper, like cleaning a foggy visor. Joy rose and stayed. Start your own count. Thank God for shoes, water, a coach who pushes you, parents who drive you, a body that heals. Watch how your shoulders lower and your smile returns. Grateful players last longer, lead better, and love deeper because their hearts keep noticing gifts.

Prayer:

Make me thankful. Open my eyes to every gift. Grow joy in me regardless of results today.

Practice:

List three blessings before practice. Tell God thanks. Share one blessing with a teammate today.

41

CONFIDENCE IS QUIET

"Let your light shine before others, that they may see your good works and glorify your Father." (Matthew 5:16)

Jonathan Isaac ties his shoes like he plays, calm and focused. No fireworks, just a steady glow. Quiet confidence is not hiding. It is knowing Who placed light inside you and why. Matthew 5:16 says shine so people see good works and praise God. That light looks like box outs when cameras blink, extra passes when points tempt, and a hand on a teammate's shoulder when heads drop. It looks like staying after to sweep the floor because someone should. Be the teammate who brings energy to warmups, talks on defense, and includes the last player in the huddle. Your light will feel like a deep river, not a loud spark. People will feel safe around you. God will get the credit.

Prayer:

Use my light for others. Make my confidence steady and my actions bright so people notice You.

Practice:

Encourage a rookie with one helpful tip and one sincere compliment after practice today.

42

FEARFULLY MADE

"We are God's workmanship, created in Christ Jesus to do good works." (Ephesians 2:10)

After film, Candace Parker tucked her daughter in and stood by the window. City lights blinked like patient fireflies. She thought about plays, then smiled about bedtime stories. God made her for both. That truth set her rhythm like a metronome. Ephesians 2:10 says you are hand crafted for good works. Your build, your style, your story are not accidents. Learn from heroes, but do not copy their footprints. Make your own with God. When you lean into your design, you stop forcing plays that do not fit and start choosing the ones that do. Peace walks with you. Look around. Where do your gifts meet someone's need. A younger player who needs guidance. A classmate who needs help. A family member who needs patience. Walk into those moments with confidence. Purpose is not someday. Purpose is today.

Prayer:

Thank You for purpose. Show me the good works You planned for me. Help me walk in them.

Practice:

Write one God given gift and one practical way to use it for your team today.

43

LIKES ARE NOT WORTH

"Each one should test their own actions, then take pride in themselves alone, without comparing." (Galatians 6:4)

Sydney McLaughlin Levrone knows the roar of a stadium and the buzz of a phone. She also knows the quiet of a screen facedown. She guards that quiet like a medal. Galatians 6:4 points her to honest self check, not public rating.
  When your joy depends on likes, your heart rides a roller coaster you cannot control. When your joy rests in faithful work, your soul walks steady ground. Do the workout. Finish the homework. Help with dishes. Stack quiet wins until confidence grows roots. Turn down the volume so you can hear God's voice. He gives steady identity and peace that lasts. Then you can post without needing applause and scroll without measuring your life against someone else's highlight.

Prayer:

Free me from comparison. Help me care more about Your voice than comments. Teach me to enjoy faithful work.

Practice:

Take a one hour screen break. Train, read Scripture, or rest in silence with God.

44

YOU ARE GOD'S MVP

"Before I formed you in the womb I knew you." (Jeremiah 1:5)

In a small Greek gym, the floor creaked like an old boat. Young Giannis dribbled with a wide grin while his brothers laughed on the sideline. No trophies. No cameras. Just love and a ball. Years later, after MVPs, he still points up first. Because the biggest prize came before any buzzer. God knew him and chose him. Jeremiah 1:5 says God knew you too. That means your value started before your first bucket, race, or grade. When you live from that truth, you stop chasing crowns to feel seen. You start using your gifts to lift people. Joy moves in and stays. So play hard. Smile often. Help your team. Whether the world notices or not, heaven already does. You are picked by the King. He never regrets His pick.

Prayer:

Use my gifts for others. Remind me I am known and chosen by You. Make my game loving.

Practice:

Post a short verse in your locker. Read it before practice. Compete remembering who chose you.

CHAPTER 4 – WHEN YOU'RE IN A SLUMP

45

ALL SLUMPS END

"Weeping may endure for a night, but joy comes in the morning." — Psalm 30:5

The crowd sounded like a storm when Clayton Kershaw left the mound. He stared at the scoreboard that felt twelve stories tall. Then he closed his eyes and pictured sunrise at an empty ballpark. Damp grass. Pink sky. A lonely bullpen with a catcher's mitt like a small planet. In that quiet memory he felt God near, like warm light on his shoulders. He remembered other dark nights that ended with coffee, Scripture, and the thump of strike after strike. One pitch is a seed. Seeds do not shout. They just grow. He rubbed the ball. Lace. Leather. Breath. He aimed not at fear, but at a tiny window on the corner, the size of a pencil eraser. Pop. Strike. His heartbeat slowed. The noise turned into ocean waves, loud but far away. Another pitch. Then another. Rhythm returned like an old friend. You know that feeling. Cold streaks in games. Bad quizzes. Social drama. Night screams forever. Morning whispers, Keep going. Your job is the next pitch. Fix your feet. Trust your training. Pray simple. God turns long nights into soft, bright mornings for anyone who keeps showing up.

Prayer:

Lord, renew my joy today. Quiet the storm in me. Steady my breath. Guide my next pitch and calm my heart.

Practice:

Write one past comeback. Thank God. Practice three basics slowly, then with game speed. Finish smiling.

46
FAILURE IS FEEDBACK

"Though the righteous fall seven times, they rise again." — Proverbs 24:16

Imagine a gym at midnight. Lights humming. A single ball echoing like a metronome. Michael Jordan misses on purpose, then rewinds the moment in his mind like a slow movie. Heel, toe, knee, elbow, wrist, snap. He takes one step back and asks the miss a question. What are you trying to teach me? Fails are like coaches that do not flatter. They tell the truth and hand you a map. Jordan prays quietly, Teach me. Then he runs a tiny experiment. Change the foot angle by one inch. Hold the follow through one heartbeat longer. Count three breaths. Swish. Not magic. Method. The miss turns into a message, the message into a drill, the drill into a habit that shows up under bright lights. Your life works the same. Bomb a test? Track the exact step you missed. Drop a pass? Study your eyes. Were they already running? Write one lesson. Only one. Then train it until it feels boring and automatic. Rising is not random. Rising is learned, rehearsed, and repeated until confidence grows like roots.

Prayer:

Lord, teach me through mistakes. Make me brave enough to review, wise enough to adjust, and strong enough to rise.

Practice:

After practice, list one mistake and one fix. Share it, drill it, and check it tomorrow.

47

YOU ARE NOT YOUR DEFEATS

"Forget the former things; do not dwell on the past. See, I am doing a new thing." — Isaiah 43:18–19

Serena Williams sat in a silent locker room. Tape on the floor. A towel like a small mountain on the bench. The loss felt heavy, like wet clothes. She breathed, opened her Bible, and the words felt like a key clicking open a door. New thing. Not fake positivity. A promise. She stood, faced a mirror, and chose one small target. Calm return. Higher toss. Softer jaw. She wrote it on a sticky note and stuck it to her water bottle like a mission badge. The next morning, the court was painted with light. She practiced the new thing until it felt like a song she could hum with her eyes closed. People only saw trophies, but God saw moments like this, where a heart lets Him rename a day. You are not your worst clip. You are not the screenshot of a mistake. You are a work God is still writing. Pick one small goal for today. Ten clean reps. Good eye contact with your coach. Encouraging words to a teammate. Progress is louder than shame when you stick with it.

Prayer:

Father, help me release yesterday. Do a new thing in me. Give me courage to begin again right now.

Practice:

Write one new goal. Pray it. Schedule it. Do one tiny step before bedtime tonight.

48

REST WITHOUT QUITTING

"Come to Me, all who are weary and burdened, and I will give you rest." — Matthew 11:28

Kevin Durant's comeback did not start with dunks. It started with ice melting in a plastic bin, bands stretching like small rainbows, and a notebook full of boring numbers. He wrote feelings as well as reps. Tight. Calm. Sharp. Tired. He read Scripture between sets and felt God's voice like a gentle coach. Slow is still forward. Rest was a bright green light, not a red stop sign. He slept with purpose, ate for healing, lifted with care, and trusted the clock he could not control. One afternoon the gym smelled like rubber and hope. His footwork looked like dance steps. Smooth. Balanced. Patient. He jogged, then cut, then rose for a jumper that sounded like a drum when it hit net. Rest made this possible. You are not a machine. God is not asking you to grind until you break. He is inviting you to trade heavy for holy. Take a Sabbath hour where you stop and let your soul breathe. Stretch slowly. Drink water like it matters. Read one Psalm. Rest is training for the inside you.

Prayer:

Jesus, give me real rest. Quiet my mind, heal my body, and reset my heart so I finish well.

Practice:

Schedule one Sabbath hour. No screens. Stretch, hydrate, read Scripture, journal three thanks, breathe slowly.

49

FAITH IN OFFSEASON

"We know that all things work together for good for those who love God."
— Romans 8:28

After the parade, the lights go down, and champions hear the whisper of empty gyms. LeBron James walks in with a notebook and a plan. The world sees posters. Offseason sees ladders, footwork, and a tiny tweak to a pivot. He counts out loud, writes numbers, and thanks God for the quiet space where no one claps and everything grows. Film sessions feel like treasure hunts. He pauses, points with a pen, and finds a better read hidden in the chaos. Your offseason might be summer, a bench stretch, or a rainy Saturday with no ride. Good. Seeds love dirt and darkness. That is where roots grab hold. Pick one lonely skill. Ten minutes every day, even if the gym echoes. Pray, Grow me. Track progress like a scientist. Little numbers turn into big moments later. Hidden work becomes visible power. Trust that God is braiding all the small choices together. When the season returns, your body will remember what your notebook recorded. Your confidence will feel like a mountain.

Prayer:

Father, grow me in the quiet. Use small daily work for good. Build my skill and my character.

Practice:

Choose one solo skill. Ten focused minutes today. Log reps, rate quality, and thank God.

50

WHEN COACH SAYS NO

"Trust in the Lord with all your heart… He will make your paths straight."
— Proverbs 3:5–6

Brock Purdy stood by a whiteboard filled with plays that looked like constellations. The coach said, Not today. The word felt like a door closing softly. Brock swallowed, nodded, and thanked him. Then he stayed. He traced routes with his finger, learned protections by heart, and threw to empty spots on the field, trusting teammates he could not see. After practice he prayed in his locker, Guide me. Delay did not shrink him. It shaped him. Weeks later, the stadium roared. Everyone else saw a surprise. Brock saw film turning into faith. Feet calm. Eyes steady. Ball out on time. The no had trained him to listen better and lead cleaner. You will hear no. It might be a cut list, a benching, or a skipped role. Let the no teach, not tattoo. Ask your coach for one focus point. Write it on your shoe. Show up early with great energy. God straightens paths for hearts that trust Him with timing.

Prayer:

Lord, guide me in delay. Keep me teachable and thankful. Make my steps straight as I trust You.

Practice:

Thank your coach. Ask for one focus. Write it somewhere visible. Train it today with full effort.

51

BOUNCE BACK 24 RULE

"His mercies are new every morning; great is Your faithfulness." — Lamentations 3:22–23

Patrick Mahomes walks to the sideline after a rough drive. He taps his chest twice, looks up, and breathes like someone opening a window. New air. New chance. In his mind he sees a clock that resets at sunrise. Twenty four hours to feel it, learn it, and then let it drift away like a balloon. He meets God in that window. Forgive me if I forced it. Thank You for fresh mercy. Show me the fix. Then he huddles and says, Next play, eyes up. You need that reset too. Bad game, weird friend group moment, tough grade. Take the lesson, not the label. Write one correction, not a whole novel. Ask forgiveness if you hurt someone. Then hand the weight to God and go to sleep like a champion. Morning arrives with soft light and strong mercy.

The 24 hour rule frees your mind, protects your joy, and lets you attack the day with clear focus.

Prayer:

Father, reset me with mercy. Help me learn quickly, forgive fully, and compete today with a clear, thankful heart.

Practice:

Use the 24 hour rule. Review, learn, confess if needed. Release it. Wake up ready.

52
FAITH OVER FRUSTRATION

"Consider it pure joy whenever you face trials, because you know the testing of your faith produces perseverance." — James 1:2–3

Katie Ledecky watches tiny bubbles slide along the lane line like silver beads. The set is long and spicy. Shoulders ache. Clock blinks cold numbers. She smiles anyway. Not a pretend smile. A choice. She thanks God for water that teaches, lungs that burn into strength, and coaches who clap at the hardest parts. Joy turns into fuel that does not run out. Stroke by stroke, the pain becomes a partner. Your practice will punch back. A drill that feels endless. A coach who keeps saying again. Choose joy like you pick up a weight. Tell your body the trial is building you, not breaking you. Pray, Mature me. Keep your head still, hands soft, eyes patient. Watch frustration melt into focus and see the clock quietly slide in your favor.

Joy is not ignoring pain. Joy is believing the pain has a purpose, and that purpose is growth you can feel.

Prayer:

Lord, mature me through trials. Give me joy that lasts, patience to endure, and wisdom to grow today.

Practice:

During the hardest drill, smile on purpose. Thank God. Keep form clean. Finish strong without quitting.

53

COMEBACK MINDSET

"We are hard pressed on every side, but not crushed; perplexed, but not in despair." — 2 Corinthians 4:8–9

Alex Smith stared at a leg wrapped like a spaceship. Doctors spoke carefully. The hill looked enormous. He decided to take it one pebble at a time. First step to the hallway. Then two. He counted victories like stars on the ceiling. He thanked God for every inch. Friends visited. Kids laughed. Hope walked in wearing sneakers. Later, a quiet field. Grass like velvet. He stood in place and practiced a simple throw. Wrist. Laces. Breath. The ball spun like a small planet returning home. Months stacked like Lego bricks. Strength returned with a shy smile. One day he ran. One day he played. His life preached a sermon without words. Pressed is not crushed when grace carries the weight. Your comeback might be an ankle, a grade, or a friendship. Start tiny. Ask God to raise your spirit, even when your body lags. Encourage someone near you. Courage grows best in groups. Let hope set your pace. Pebbles turn into paths.

Prayer:

Jesus, raise me up. When I feel pressed, hold me. Give me courage, patience, and steady steps today.

Practice:

Encourage an injured teammate. Send a voice note, pray for them, and check in after practice.

54

INVISIBLE BUT SEEN

"The Lord is close to the brokenhearted and saves those who are crushed in spirit." — Psalm 34:18

The bench can feel like the moon. You wave from far away while others dance in sunlight. You warm up, sit, and wonder if anyone notices. God does. He saw David with sheep and saw you with a clipboard. You decide to turn the bench into a lab. You watch feet. You track tendencies. You call out back screens like a lighthouse. When teammates come off, you tap fists and name something specific they did well.

One game, the coach whispers your name. You jog in already sweating from cheering. Your heart is calm because you have been playing the whole time in your head. Quick stop. Smart pass. Box out. The crowd roars for the score, but Heaven smiles for the faithfulness that built it. If you feel invisible, tell God the truth. He is near to honest hearts. Let Him remind you who you are. Not a seat number. A servant leader. Stay ready. Celebrate others. Trust His timing.

Prayer:

Lord, see me here. Fill me with purpose on the bench. Give me joy to serve and stay ready.

Practice:

Cheer specifically. Call screens, celebrate effort, write two film notes, and encourage one teammate by name.

55
GRIT IS GROWN

"Suffering produces perseverance; perseverance, character; and character, hope." — Romans 5:3–4

Naomi Osaka stepped away to heal. Silence became a new coach. She learned to breathe like waves, slow and steady. She wrote prayers on sticky notes by her mirror. One said, Purpose over pressure. When she returned, her game had a quiet center, like a lake at sunrise. Grit was not a mood. It was a garden she watered with small faithful choices.

Hard days still came, but she did not panic. She planted. Finish the drill. Hydrate. Stretch. Journal one truth. Encourage one person. Those seeds grew roots. Roots became strength. Strength became hope that did not wobble every time the wind blew.

You do not have to like pain to use it. Ask God to grow perseverance in you, one clean decision at a time. Do the homework. Finish the rep. Turn off the phone earlier. Kindness counts as strength too. Character stacks like bricks, and hope moves in to live there.

Prayer:

God, grow grit in me. Help me be patient and steady. Use hard moments to build strong, hopeful character.

Practice:

Push one extra minute next drill. Focus on form. Breathe rhythm. Finish with a grateful heart.

56

FAITH THROUGH FATIGUE

"Those who hope in the Lord will renew their strength." — Isaiah 40:31

Eliud Kipchoge runs like a poem. Shoes kiss the road. Arms swing like metronomes. When fatigue presses, he does not fight wild. He waits wisely. He listens for the quiet voice inside that says, Not yet. He prays while moving. Thank You for breath. Thank You for legs. He saves his surge like a secret kept in his pocket. Then at the right moment, he opens it.

You have days where your body feels like wet cement. Before practice, sit for two minutes. No music. Just you and God. Tell Him exactly how you feel. Ask for strength that is not from a can. Then train with patience. Set your pace. Keep your form clean. Choose calm over chaos. Renewal belongs to hopers, not hurry. When you finish, look back and notice the strength that arrived while you waited.

Prayer:

Lord, renew me today. Meet me in my fatigue. Give me patient strength and a peaceful mind to finish well.

Practice:

Take a slow prayer walk. Inhale Scripture, exhale worry. Return ready and steady for training.

57
NEVER TAP OUT

"My grace is sufficient for you, for My power is made perfect in weakness."
— 2 Corinthians 12:9

Tua Tagovailoa has heard the doubts. He has felt the sting of injuries. On tough days he sits with a Bible and a notebook. He writes the verse like a helmet for his mind. My grace is enough. He tells God where it hurts and lets weakness be a window, not a wall. Grace floods in like light through open blinds. He plays looser, hears teammates clearer, and leads with a smile that rests instead of pretends.

You do not need to be unbreakable. You need to be honest. Say the hard thing in prayer. I am scared. I am exhausted. I messed up. Then listen. God meets weakness with power you can feel. Memorize the verse so it will meet you mid drill. One step. One pass. One quiet act of courage. Grace will carry what your muscles cannot.

Prayer:

Jesus, be my power. I bring You my weakness. Fill me with grace, courage, and peace so I keep going.

Practice:

Memorize this verse today. Repeat it during drills and games until your heart believes it.

58
LESSON IN LOSING

"Listen to advice and accept instruction, that you may gain wisdom in the future." — Proverbs 19:20

The USWNT's 2023 exit felt like a cold wave. Cameras caught tears, then arms around shoulders, then a long walk to the locker room where the room smelled like grass and quiet. Later, film. Pause. Rewind. Play. Coaches asked hard questions with soft voices. Players spoke honestly. Pride took a seat so wisdom could stand. Losing became a classroom, not a cage.

You will lose too. A meet slips away. A part goes to someone else. Do not scroll it numb. Ask your coach for one clear adjustment. Journal it like a promise. Pray, Teach me. Then practice the correction until it feels like muscle music. God does not waste pain. He turns honest reflection into sharper choices. Tomorrow's edge is often hiding inside today's bruise. When the next chance comes, you will feel calmer. You will recognize the moment because you studied it in the dark.

Prayer:

Father, teach me through loss. Give me humility to listen, courage to change, and hope to try again.

Practice:

After the game, write one lesson. Share it with a teammate. Drill it tomorrow with focus.

CHAPTER 5 - THE REAL GAME

59

PLAY CLEAN

"The Lord detests lying lips, but He delights in people who are trustworthy."
Proverbs 12:22

The dugout lights hummed like bees. Chalk floated in the warm night air. Shohei Ohtani tapped his bat and looked down the foul line, where a tiny breeze carried the popcorn smell from the stands. He had guessed the pitch last at-bat and felt the tug to peek at a sign. He didn't. He breathed, stepped in, and chose honesty over an easy edge. Later, alone in the tunnel, he listened to his spikes click on concrete and felt light inside, like windows opening. Trustworthy. That word felt like a clean jersey. He pictured little lies that stain seasons. Feet sliding early on sprints. Reps you say you finished but didn't. A secret glance for advantage. Those shortcuts feel powerful for a second, then heavy. Truth feels slow for a second, then fast. Shohei decided integrity would be his pregame: stretch, breathe, pray, play clean. Your field is the same. Pick truth on the tiny things. Your heart gets quiet, your focus sharpens, and your joy runs free.

Prayer:

Lord, make me honest today. Clean my motives, my mouth, and my habits, so my game and my name bring You delight.

Practice:

Tell a trusted person one shortcut you took. Fix it now, then choose the honest read all practice.

60

OWN MISTAKES

"If we confess our sins, He is faithful and just and will forgive us our sins." 1 John 1:9

Stadium noise still clung to the air when Derek Carr sat with the tablet. One red-zone throw sailed high, and the whole place gasped. He could feel the easy excuses forming like storm clouds. Wind. Timing. Turf. Instead he walked to his coach, looked him in the eyes, and said, "That was on me." The words felt like a door clicking open. In the film room, a yellow circle paused over his late read. He whispered, "Forgive me," and then, "Teach me." Feet, eyes, timing. He drilled the fix until muscle memory sang. Next game, same play, ball snapped, eyes calm, completion made. The locker room felt lighter because truth was normal. Confession is not a spotlight on your failure. It is a switch that turns on learning. God meets truth with mercy, not a hammer. Your life is the same. Own it fast, fix it slow, smile sooner. That is how trust grows and wins return.

Prayer:

Jesus, forgive me quickly. Help me speak truth, accept correction, learn the lesson, and walk forward clean and confident.

Practice:

Tell someone you wronged, "I messed up." Ask, "How can I repair this," then take the first step today.

61
HUMILITY WINS

"In humility value others above yourselves, not looking to your own interests but each of you to the interests of others." Philippians 2:3-4

Third period, tie game, legs burning. Matt Duchene, NHL forward known for speed, creativity, and a Christian faith, flew down the wing. He could rip the shot and chase glory. Instead he spotted a teammate slip behind the defense. Quick fake, crisp pass, tape to tape. Goal. Crowd exploded. Duchene pointed at his linemate and tapped his chest, That was you.

Serving the team first will not make you smaller. It makes your influence larger. Coaches trust you. Teammates skate harder beside you. Humility sharpens vision. You notice the open man, the loose puck, the tired friend. You stop needing to be the star and start making stars. At school this looks like setting a screen, diving for a save that helps another score, or sharing a tip that improved your shot. It looks like apologizing fast and sharing credit. Pray, "Keep me low," before games. Low is not weak. It is strength that lifts. Assist first. Celebrate others. God sees. Teams that serve each other become hard to beat..

Prayer:

Lord, Jesus, keep me low. Give me eyes to serve, courage to pass, quick apologies, and joy when others score. Amen.

Practice:

Pick a teammate to set up today. Ask how to help them score or shine.

62

EGO VS EXCELLENCE

"Pride goes before destruction, a haughty spirit before a fall." Proverbs 16:18

Flashbulbs blinked like stars as Cam Newton adjusted his chin strap. There was a stretch when swagger got louder than study. He hunted highlight throws and forgot footwork. Film is honest. It paused on lazy eyes and drifting feet. In a quiet room that smelled like marker and coffee, Cam felt the sting, then the invitation. He chose excellence over ego. Feet first. Eyes disciplined. Progressions counted like beats in a song. Practice turned into music again. Teammates leaned in because humility made space for them. Coaches smiled because corrections stuck. Pride is a glittery trap. It promises, then trips you. Excellence is a simple path. It whispers, then lifts you. You face the same choice in math class, workouts, even group chats. Do you want attention or improvement. Compliment a rival's good play today. Let it remind you that greatness has teachers everywhere. Ego stares at mirrors. Excellence studies film and gets better.

Prayer:

Father, guard my heart from pride. Give me courage to accept correction, do details well, and choose growth over attention.

Practice:

Praise a rival's skill out loud. Then pick one detail to fix today and practice it with full focus.

63

BE COACHABLE

"Listen to advice and accept discipline, and at the end you will be counted among the wise." Proverbs 19:20

The huddle felt electric. Patrick Mahomes leaned in until his facemask nearly bumped the whiteboard. He repeated the play softly like a prayer, then jogged out grinning. Coachability is speed you cannot time. It turns somebody else's years of learning into your next good decision. After practice, the field smelled like cut grass and effort. Patrick asked, "One thing to clean today." The answer was tiny, and that is the magic. Little turns move big ships. He wrote it on tape around his wrist, then drilled it until sunset. Wisdom comes to the athlete who listens. You do not have to love criticism, just invite it and use it. Coaches risk more with players who hear. Friends speak truth to people who do not snap back. If you want a higher ceiling, lower your guard. Ask, write, repeat, apply. You will feel your mind quiet and your game sharpen.

Prayer:

God, open my ears. Help me welcome correction, remember it, and practice it until wisdom becomes my daily habit.

Practice:

Ask a coach or captain for one specific fix. Write it down. Apply it on the very next rep.

64

HONEST EYES

"The eye is the lamp of the body. If your eyes are healthy, your whole body will be full of light." Matthew 6:22

Night air glowed around the stadium as Abby Wambach scanned the box. Her eyes were hungry, but clean. No peeking at signals. No jersey tugs. She trusted her vision and her work. Healthy eyes are more than eyesight. They are choices. After matches, phone in hand, Abby guarded her feed like a goal. If it dimmed her heart, she scrolled past. If it brightened courage, she lingered. Jesus said light enters through your eyes. What you watch becomes your wind. Cheat clips teach shortcuts. Truth clips teach grit. On the field, honest eyes notice the late run, the open lane, the ref's angle. Off the field, honest eyes choose what builds, not what breaks. You can train your gaze. Curate your scroll. Stare at technique, not trash. Look long at Scripture, then look long at your teammates. Light gets in, choices brighten, and your steps feel fast again.

Prayer:

Jesus, purify my eyes. Protect my focus. Fill me with light so my choices and play stay honest and brave.

Practice:

Choose truth with your eyes today. No cheating, no shady content. Look for what builds and follow it.

65

APOLOGIZE LIKE A PRO

"Bear with each other and forgive one another if any of you has a grievance. Forgive as the Lord forgave you." Colossians 3:13

The practice field sounded like drums, pads thumping in rhythm. Damar Hamlin flowed through a drill and clipped a teammate during a thud period. Whistle chirped. He jogged over, helmet off, eyes clear. "I am sorry. You good." The apology was simple, but it moved the air. Shoulders dropped. Tension melted. Grace is a healer. Later, in the locker room, the smell of tape and detergent hung in the air. Damar thought about second chances and the God who gives them. Real apologies are not speeches. They are doors. You open them with honest words, and then you walk through with changed behavior. Say it without excuses, then prove it with safer play, softer tone, better habits. Your team learns to breathe again. You learn to listen faster. Forgiveness keeps a season from cracking under pressure. Practice it now so it is ready when games get loud.

Prayer:

Lord, help me forgive and be forgiven. Make my words honest, my posture gentle, and my follow-through different.

Practice:

Say sorry to someone you bumped, snapped at, or ignored. Add one action that repairs trust today.

66
RESPECT THE RULES

"Let everyone be subject to the governing authorities, for there is no authority except that which God has established." Romans 13:1

The clock hit warmup and Nick Saban's whistle sang. Lines straight. Helmets buckled. No flinch. His practices feel like a train running on perfectly laid tracks. Rules are not cages. They are rails that carry you faster. When athletes fight rules, the train wobbles. When they honor them, momentum roars. You may not love every call or curfew, but respect builds trust. Trust builds opportunity. Opportunity builds influence. Saban's phrase is simple: Do your job. That job might be sprinting through the line, lifting with full reps, or wearing what the team requires. In the wider world it looks like showing up early, turning in clean work, and honoring parents and teachers. Order makes room for excellence. Chaos eats energy. Choose order and watch your mind calm. You will play faster because your decisions ride on rails.

Prayer:

God, teach me respect. Help me honor leaders, follow team rules, and bring order that blesses everyone around me.

Practice:

Pick one rule you often bend. Keep it perfectly all week. Tell a teammate and let them hold you accountable.

67
WIN WITH CLASS

"Do not repay evil with evil or insult with insult. On the contrary, repay evil with blessing." 1 Peter 3:8-9

The trophy's silver caught the arena lights like sunrise on water. Roger Federer wiped his face with a towel, nodded to the crowd, and thanked ball kids by name. His voice was soft, but it carried. Class is quiet power. It says, "I know who I am, so I do not need to crush you with words." After matches, Roger praised the other player's fight and effort. That lifted the whole sport. Scripture tells us to bless, not swing back. On your court that looks like a handshake first, a kind word to officials, and a thank you to the trainer who re-taped your ankle. It looks like celebrating without taunting and posting without rubbing it in. People remember how you made them feel. Class turns opponents into iron that sharpens you. Win with grace and your reputation becomes sturdy, not flashy. Trophies tarnish. Character shines.

Prayer:

Lord, keep me kind when I win. Give me grateful words, a gentle posture, and respect for everyone who helped.

Practice:

After a win, handshake first. Thank opponents, officials, and staff. Share credit before photos or posts.

68

LOSE WITHOUT EXCUSE

"Let someone else praise you, and not your own mouth." Proverbs 27:2

The camera light blinked red while Albert Pujols rubbed the dirt from his palms. Hitless night. Questions coming. He smiled small. "Their pitcher was sharp. I will work." No wind story. No zone complaint. Later, in a quiet cage that smelled like pine tar and focus, he chased the fix with steady swings. Losing without excuses is not weakness. It is courage. It clears the fog so you can see the next step. Proverbs tells us not to brag ourselves up; let results speak later. When you drop excuses, you pick up tools. Film. Reps. Rest. Honesty. Your teammates relax because drama leaves the room. Your coaches invest because truth lives in you. The next time contact returns and the ball jumps, people know it came from real work, not loud talk. Your heart will know it too, and peace will settle in your chest.

Prayer:

God, help me own losses. Remove excuses from my mouth. Teach me to learn quickly and return stronger.

Practice:

If you fail today, say, "I will learn," then start one small improvement within the next hour.

69
ADMIT WEAKNESS

"My grace is sufficient for you, for My power is made perfect in weakness."
2 Corinthians 12:9

The rim looked smaller than usual. Steph Curry bounced the ball, breathed, and felt that tight band of frustration around his chest. In film he raised his hand first. "I need help here." In the training room he said, "This muscle feels off." Weakness confessed did not make him smaller. It made space for God's strength and the team's wisdom. Paul says power is perfected in weakness. That means your honesty becomes the doorway where grace walks in. After practice, the gym smelled like rubber and hope. Steph stayed, but not to prove he was fine. He stayed to practice the right fixes. Shots began to sound sweet again. You can do this in your hallway and huddle. Tell a mentor where anxiety grabs you. Ask for a drill, a verse, a plan. God meets need with supply, and peace returns before the makes do.

Prayer:

Lord, use my weakness. Give me courage to ask for help, receive grace, and keep practicing with hope.

Practice:

Share one struggle with a trusted adult. Ask for one drill or step, then do it today.

70
TEMPTATION TIMEOUT

"God is faithful. He will not let you be tempted beyond what you can bear, but will also provide a way out." 1 Corinthians 10:13

Josh Hamilton learned to stack exits like stairs. Before pressure showed up, he wrote escape routes on a card in his bag. Call a friend. Step outside. Pray for sixty seconds. Drive home. Temptation loves surprise and shadows. Plans bring light. One night, the laughter felt too wild and the music too sticky. He slipped to the porch, breathed cool air, dialed a safe number, and walked toward peace. God promises a way out. It might feel small, like choosing water, muting a chat, or giving your phone to a parent for an hour, but small doors lead to big freedom. Your brain rewires when you choose escape over excuse. Shame shrinks. Strength grows. Write your exits now, while you are calm, and keep them close. When the moment comes, you will not guess. You will go.

Prayer:

Jesus, rescue me fast. Show the escape path quickly, give me courage to take it, and friends to walk with me.

Practice:

List three escape routes for your biggest temptation. Keep them visible and use one the very next time.

71
BE REAL

"You will know the truth, and the truth will set you free." John 8:32

Jayson Tatum stared at the ceiling of a quiet gym, then rolled up to shoot again. Rough night. Heavy legs. Instead of posting a filtered clip, he filmed the sweat, the misses, the work. Caption: Back to it. People felt seen. Truth does that. It opens the windows and lets fresh air in. When you tell the truth about your grades, your minutes, your feelings, you stop guarding an image and start growing a life. Coaches can coach you. Friends can help you. God already knows and loves you. The lie promises protection and delivers pressure. The truth feels scary for a moment and then light floods the room. Be real with a teacher about an assignment you blew. Be real with a parent about a text thread that got messy. Speak it, then take the next right step. Freedom sounds like a deep breath after rain.

Prayer:

Lord, keep me real today. Put truth in my mouth, courage in my heart, and freedom in my steps.

Practice:

Share one honest update with someone safe. Ask for support, then take one clear action forward.

72
PLAY FOR GOD'S GLORY

"Whether you eat or drink or whatever you do, do it all for the glory of God."
1 Corinthians 10:31

Eric Liddell said he felt God's pleasure when he ran, like wind lifting a kite. On the track he lifted his chin, relaxed his shoulders, and flowed. The crowd sounded distant, like ocean waves, and his heartbeat felt like worship. Playing for God's glory does not make competition smaller. It makes your why bigger. Pressure changes shape. The scoreboard matters, but it does not own you. Warmups can become prayer. Effort becomes a gift you hand back to the One who gave breath. Before practice, whisper, "This is Yours." Then sprint with clean play, brave love, and a thankful spirit. People will notice a different shine. Wins taste sweeter. Losses do not crush you. Your identity stops wobbling with every stat. You are free to run in the lane God gave you and smile while you do it.

Prayer:

Father, receive my game. I give You my effort, attitude, and outcomes. Let my play honor You today.

Practice:

Pray before practice. Thank God for breath, body, teammates, coaches, and a fresh chance to compete with joy.

73
POWER OF WE

"Two are better than one, because they have a good return for their labor."
Ecclesiastes 4:9

The Warriors were down late, the crowd tense. Then a tiny spark. A bench wing sprinted to screen. A big dove on the floor to save a loose ball. Steph pointed. Draymond clapped. Klay nodded. Five players moved with one heartbeat, and a run began. Shots fell. Rotations clicked. The building shook. After the buzzer, reporters asked about the hero. They smiled and said, "All of us."
Unity is not perfect people. It is committed people. The Warriors practice talking early, celebrating screens, owning mistakes, and covering for each other. Ecclesiastes says two are better than one. Courts and fields prove it nightly.
Your team may not have banners, but you can bring the glue. Sit by the quiet kid. High five the sub. Call out picks. Unity grows through small choices that say we before me. When you bind together, pressure gets lighter and wins get louder. Champions are not the strongest individuals. They are the tightest groups. Choose that today and watch everything change.

Prayer:

Lord, bind us together in purpose and love. Make me unselfish, attentive, brave to protect and uplift teammates today, always.

Practice:

Text one teammate encouragement, ask a need, then follow through quietly after practice this week.

74

ENCOURAGE EACH OTHER

"Consider how to spur one another on toward love and good deeds." Hebrews 10:24

Tony Dungy coached with calm strength. In a noisy league, his words were steady and careful. After a tough loss, he found a player, looked him in the eye, and spoke life. "You belong here. Keep doing the right things." That voice built teams that kept working. Encouragement did not make them soft. It made them strong enough to grow. Hebrews says to consider how to spur others on. That means plan your words like a play. Dungy did not wait for perfect moments. He created them with simple praise and clear next steps. You can do this today. Stop a teammate after drills. "I saw your hustle. Keep that energy." Text the injured kid, "We need you." Cheer effort more than points. When your words chase people toward good, God's purpose shows up at practice. Encouragement is free, but it multiplies like wild. Give it away until the room sounds different and hearts start to rise.

Prayer:

Lord, use my words to lift others. Help me notice effort, speak hope, correct kindly, and point teammates toward You.

Practice:

Send one short text today. Praise something specific. Offer help this week. Follow up after practice.

75

RESPECT THE COACH

"Obey your leaders and submit to them, for they keep watch over your souls."
Hebrews 13:17

Nick Saban talks about the Process. Reps done right. Eyes up. Details matter. Players say the hardest part is not the sprints. It is choosing to trust instruction when pride gets loud. Respect is not blind. It is disciplined. You listen, ask, learn, and do what is asked with full effort. That posture turns average athletes into dependable leaders. Hebrews reminds us leaders carry weight for the group. Your coach might be fiery or quiet. Not every decision will feel perfect. But choosing respect brings order, and order unlocks growth. Ask good questions. Make eye contact. Hustle to the huddle. Own your role without eye rolls. Respect does not mean you never share concerns. It means you share them the right way, at the right time, with the right tone. When you honor authority, you honor God. The whole team moves smoother and stronger because trust clears the lane for everyone.

Prayer:

Lord, humble me. Help me honor coaches, learn quickly, accept correction, and give full effort even when I disagree.

Practice:

Thank your coach after practice. Ask, "One thing to improve tomorrow?" Write it down, review, and do it.

76
CHEER THE BENCH

"Look not only to your own interests, but also to the interests of others."
Philippians 2:4

The best noise in gyms usually starts on the bench. Clapping rises. Players jump for a teammate's shot. Someone yells after a charge. Benched players choose joy for others. That choice changes teams. When the horn sounds and your number is not called, you still have a job. Eyes on the floor. Celebrate the sub. Call out screens. Meet scorers with towels and smiles. Philippians tells us to look to others. That is hard when you want minutes. But cheering is not fake. It is a battle against jealousy. It reminds your heart the team is bigger than your stat line. Coaches notice. Teammates feel it. Chemistry grows. Be that energy. Decide before the game, "I will make the bench a bonfire." Your moment will come, and you will enter already focused and giving. Joy for others prepares you for your chance and builds a culture where everyone gets better together.

Prayer:

Lord, make me generous. Teach me to celebrate others, fight jealousy, and bring loud, steady joy from the first whistle.

Practice:

Choose one benched teammate to celebrate. Stand, clap, shout their best play every quarter today.

77

SERVE BEFORE SHINE

"Whoever wants to be first must be servant of all." Mark 9:35

Tim Tebow's highlight reels show touchdowns and trophies, but teammates remember the unseen things. Picking up trash in the locker room. Helping a freshman learn protections. Staying for photos with kids long after games. Serving did not shrink his impact. It grew it. People listen to leaders who carry water before they carry speeches. Jesus sets the blueprint. Greatness begins with a towel. When you serve, pride gets quiet and purpose gets loud. Do the hidden chore. Clean the bus aisle. Fill the water rack. Ask a manager how to help. Smile while you do it. Serving trains your heart to notice needs and move first. It builds trust. When your time comes to shine, people will already know you care more about the team than your name. That kind of leader can challenge others and be heard. Start small today. Stack secret acts. God sees and shapes you into someone strong enough to handle a brighter stage.

Prayer:

Lord, make me servant. Give me eyes for needs, quick hands to help, and a happy heart to serve.

Practice:

Find one hidden job today. Do it fully and quietly. Thank the person who usually does it.

78

BE THE ENERGY

"Whatever you do, do it in the name of the Lord Jesus." Colossians 3:17

Steph Curry plays with bright joy that spreads. The shimmy after a big shot. The smile during warmups. The way he lifts fans and teammates with simple fun. That energy is not fake. It is chosen. It starts in gratitude to God for the chance to compete. Colossians says do everything in Jesus' name. That turns energy into worship. You do not wait to feel hype. You bring it. You lead the warm-up line with a grin. You clap for effort. You keep spirits up when shots miss. Energy is a skill. Sleep well. Hydrate. Speak life. Make eye contact. Laugh at yourself. Your joy will loosen tight shoulders and free good play. When the star and the sub both feel valued, the gym brightens. Decide to be that spark today. Not loud and showy, but steady, playful, and locked in. Joy makes teams dangerous and practice a place people want to be.

Prayer:

Lord, brighten my team. Fill me with grateful joy that lifts attitudes, fuels effort, and honors You in everything.

Practice:

Lead warmups smiling. High five everyone. Start a simple chant that celebrates hustle more than points.

79
FORGIVE FAST

"Be kind and compassionate to one another, forgiving each other." Ephesians 4:32

Grant Williams once fouled hard, then offered a hand and a word. The game stayed intense, but the temperature dropped. Forgiveness is not weakness. It is control. When you forgive fast, you refuse to let anger coach you. Ephesians calls us to be kind and compassionate. That matters when a teammate misses you on a cut or an opponent talks trash. Take a breath. Say, "We got the next one." Reset your face and your feet. Forgiveness repairs chemistry before it cracks. It protects focus. It teaches your heart to choose team over ego. Hold grudges and you get heavy legs. Release them and you play free. Make it a habit. Apologize quick when you mess up. Accept apologies without drama. Pray for a soft heart. Games turn on tiny edges. A clear mind might be the edge that wins the day. Choose mercy at game speed and watch your team breathe easier.

Prayer:

Lord, soften me. Teach me to forgive quickly, apologize humbly, and compete with a clear mind and calm heart.

Practice:

Drop one grudge today. Tell the person, "We are good," then back it with kind action.

80

UNITY WINS

"How good and pleasant it is when God's people live together in unity."
Psalm 133:1

The Kansas City Chiefs are known for creative plays and loud fans, but their true edge is trust. Receivers block for each other. Linemen celebrate touchdowns. Stars teach rookies. That unity shows up when games get tight. Everyone believes the next guy will handle his job.
Psalm 133 says unity is good and pleasant. It also wins. You build it by sharing credit, serving, and staying connected off the field. Eat together. Pray together. Laugh together. Correct with respect. When unity grows, fear shrinks. Players stop hiding. They play fast because love removes the need to protect your image. That is powerful. Bring that to your team. Start a short prayer circle. Invite the new kid to sit with you. Listen well. Unity is built one brave invitation at a time, and it turns a group of players into a family that can handle storms.

Prayer:

Lord, unite us. Help us protect each other, share credit, and fight for one another with patient, joyful love.

Practice:

Invite teammates to a brief huddle after practice. Thank God together and ask for help to serve.

81

SPEAK LIFE

"Death and life are in the power of the tongue." Proverbs 18:21

Russell Wilson is known for steady positivity. In huddles and hallways, he chooses words that lift. That does not mean ignoring mistakes. It means naming truth with hope. "We can fix this." "I trust you." Those words change body language and effort. Proverbs says the tongue holds life or death. On a team, that is obvious. One complaint can poison a locker room. One word of belief can flip a game. Choose your side. Decide your phrases before pressure hits. "Next play." "Great screen." "Proud of your fight." Then use them when it is hard. Learn to praise effort, not just results. Your voice can become a bell that calls people back to focus and faith. God can use your mouth to move hearts and momentum.

Prayer:

Lord, control my tongue. Put life in my words, truth with kindness, and courage to speak when silence harms.

Practice:

Catch one complaint today. Replace it with a specific praise or a solution within five seconds.

82

CELEBRATE OTHERS

"Rejoice with those who rejoice." Romans 12:15

When Allyson Felix won medals, she smiled wide. When a teammate won, she cheered just as hard. That is maturity. Joy that is not jealous grows teams like sunlight. Romans tells us to rejoice with the rejoicing. That means when a friend PRs, you celebrate even if your day was rough.

Practice this: run to the teammate who scored, shout their name, mean it. Post their highlight before yours. Tell the starter, "I love how you prepared." Your heart will feel lighter.

Celebration is contagious. Soon the whole locker room will race to be first to clap for someone else. The atmosphere changes. People risk more. They know their wins will be welcomed, not resented. That is the kind of culture God loves to bless. Choose to be a loud echo of good news today and watch joy spread across your team.

Prayer:

Lord, make me glad for others. Remove jealousy, fill me with sincere celebration, and help me cheer every good gift.

Practice:

Give one loud, specific shoutout today for a teammate's effort, not only their stat.

83
RESPECT ALL

"So in everything, do to others what you would have them do to you."
Matthew 7:12

Serena Williams dominated with power and poise. Yet watch her greet opponents at the net, thank ball kids, and honor the rules. That is respect. It does not depend on the scoreboard. It is who you are. Jesus gives a simple rule. Treat others how you want to be treated. That means play hard without cheap shots. Shake hands with real eye contact. Thank refs even when calls sting. Speak to opponents like fellow image-bearers, not enemies. Respect does not make you soft. It frees you to compete with a clean heart. When the match ends, your character still stands. Teammates will trust you. Coaches will vouch for you. God sees, and He is honored. Train for strength and for honor. Both are part of greatness.

Prayer:

Lord, give me respect. Help me honor opponents, officials, teammates, and myself with effort, honesty, courage, and steady self-control.

Practice:

Compliment a rival after competition. Name a skill they do well and wish them well.

84
HANDLE CONFLICT

"Blessed are the peacemakers, for they will be called children of God."
Matthew 5:9

JJ Redick built a career on shooting and straight talk. Teammates say he also handled conflict quickly. If tension rose, he pulled a player aside, listened, and spoke clearly. No gossip. No delay. That made teams tighter.
 Jesus blesses peacemakers. Notice it is not peace-wishers. Peacemakers move first. When a teammate snaps at you, ask for a quick talk after practice. Use "I" statements. "I felt disrespected earlier. I want to work it out." Listen. Apologize where needed. Offer a plan.
 Peacemaking is brave. It takes humility. But it saves seasons. It turns small cracks into stronger bonds. Be that person. Your team needs a calm, honest bridge-builder who refuses to let bitterness grow. God will meet you in that hard first step and bring peace.

Prayer:

Lord, make me peace. Give me courage to address conflict gently, listen well, forgive quickly, and protect unity every day.

Practice:

Resolve one small tension today. Speak privately, listen fully, agree on a next step.

85

LIFT THE LOCKER ROOM

"Encourage one another and build each other up." 1 Thessalonians 5:11

LeBron James mentors like he scores, steady and intentional. He learns teammates' stories, remembers small details, and speaks belief into their roles. That is leadership. It is not just big speeches. It is daily construction, brick by brick, word by word. Thessalonians tells us to build up. Start with names. Ask about family. Notice effort. Send the rookie a clip of a good screen. Tell the senior you appreciate their grit. Celebrate the trainer who keeps everyone healthy. When people feel seen, they grow. The locker room warms. Hard days become possible because someone cares. Be that builder. Show up early to ask, "How can I help today?" Pray for eyes to notice. God can turn your simple encouragement into a foundation for the whole team's confidence.

Prayer:

Lord, use me to uplift. Help me notice, encourage, and invest in every person in our locker room.

Practice:

Encourage a rookie today. Share one tip, one compliment, and one invitation to work together.

86

TEAM FIRST

"By this everyone will know you are my disciples, if you love one another."
John 13:35

Tim Duncan rarely chased headlines. He set strong screens, boxed out, and passed from double teams. The Spurs' banners hang because of that quiet love for teammates. Jesus says love proves we follow Him. On teams, love looks like unselfish play. Choose the assist over a forced shot. Make the extra rotation. Help a teammate up before you celebrate.
  Team-first players are trusted in the final minute. Coaches know they will make the right read. Teammates know they will share both the ball and the blame. That kind of love is powerful. It makes everyone braver because they know they are not alone.
 Decide today to play for we, not me. Ask, "What helps us most right now?" Then do it with joy. That choice might not trend online, but it will build something that lasts and proves your faith in action.

Prayer:

Lord, grow our love. Teach me to choose the best play for the team over my own spotlight.

Practice:

In scrimmage, hunt an assist over a shot. Praise the scorer and the screener equally.

CHAPTER 7 – FINISH FAITHFULLY

87

AUDIENCE OF ONE

"Whatever you do, work at it with all your heart, as working for the Lord, not for humans." Colossians 3:23

The lights bloom like sunrise and the court shines clean as glass. Steph Curry catches a pass and the ball hums in his hands like a warm secret. Splash. The crowd erupts. Yet his mind flashes back to a tiny church gym where the floor squeaked and the hoop rattled. He was a skinny kid then, counting dribbles, whispering a simple line before every shot, My audience is You. No cameras, only echoes. He learned to chase God's smile more than the crowd's shout. That switch changed everything. When he misses, he breathes and grins. When he hits, he points up and keeps moving. Colossians 3:23 turns pressure into purpose. Play like Jesus is sitting on the baseline, cheering more for your effort and attitude than any stat. On your court, hallway, bus seat, do the same. Hustle becomes worship. Kindness becomes a highlight. Fear loses volume. Freedom steps in like a new song, and the game feels light again.

Prayer:

Lord, today I play for You alone. Quiet every loud voice inside me. Fill my effort with love, courage, and joy.

Practice:

Before warmups, touch your chest and whisper, My audience is You. Compete hard, then thank God afterward.

88

GRATITUDE IS FUEL

"Give thanks in all circumstances; for this is God's will for you in Christ Jesus." 1 Thessalonians 5:18

Chlorine hangs in the air like fog. Katie Ledecky slides into the pool and the water folds around her like silk. After a brutal set, lungs burning, she rests at the wall. Coach says, Three thanks. She stares at ripples trembling like tiny diamonds and names them out loud. Clean water. Strong legs. A friend laughing in lane three. Her shoulders drop. The next dive feels lighter. Gratitude does not delete pain. It puts a lamp in the tunnel so you can see where to place your feet. Before big races Katie whispers, Thank You, and courage rises like warm air. God asks us to give thanks because thanksgiving trains our eyes. Try it on your hardest day. Thank Him for breath, for learning, for another rep to grow. Suddenly mistakes become notes, not insults. Pressure loosens its grip. The lane becomes a place to worship, not worry, and joy starts to flow like current.

Prayer:

Father, open my eyes to gifts I miss. Thank You for strength, coaches, teammates, and small mercies that carry me.

Practice:

Write three thanks before practice. Whisper Thank You at go time. Share one gratitude with a teammate.

89

PURPOSE OVER POPULARITY

"Many are the plans in a person's heart, but it is the Lord's purpose that prevails." Proverbs 19:21

Phone glow. Comments scroll like falling rain. After a rough game, Kirk Cousins felt each word stick like burrs on a sock. He clicked, scrolled, sank. Then he closed the app and opened his Bible. Proverbs 19:21 shone like a streetlight. God's purpose stands. He prayed, Keep me focused, and drew a little play in his notebook. Not a route. A routine. Film when it is boring. Encouragement when it is awkward. Truth when it costs. Next game he walked in calm, like an anchor had dropped inside him. Not flawless, but free. You know the tug. Post this. Wear that. Chase laughs at lunch. Here is better. Ask, Does this honor God and help someone? Choose slow character over fast applause. Purpose is a compass when the hallway feels wild. It steadies your feet, clears your brain, and keeps your heart warm even when the crowd goes cold.

Prayer:

Lord, align my heart to Your purpose. Quiet the noise. Help me choose obedience over applause in every choice.

Practice:

Before you post, pray Keep me focused. Share something kind and true, or keep it in drafts.

90
FAITH THROUGH FINALS

"I have fought the good fight, I have finished the race, I have kept the faith."
2 Timothy 4:7

Blocks cold beneath her fingers, stadium humming like a giant beehive, Allyson Felix stares down a bright ribbon of track. The gun has not fired, but a lifetime lives in her legs. Rehab rooms. Baby cries. Midnight prayers. When the moment comes, she lifts her eyes and remembers who ran with her in the dark. Pop. She moves. Knees snap high. Form smooth as handwriting. Every stride says, God carried me here. The line rushes like a bright horizon and she leans through with peace. Finals are not only speed. They are faith finishing its sentence. You have finals too. Championship pressure. Chemistry exams. Tryouts with clipboards. Paul's verse is a map. Fight clean. Finish strong. Keep faith when nerves roar. When doubts crowd your lane, pray, Help me endure, and picture Jesus clapping at the finish like family. One step, then another. You do not need perfect. You need faithful. That is victory.

Prayer:

Jesus, when pressure rises, steady my breath. Strengthen my mind, guard my heart, and help me finish with faith.

Practice:

After practice, replay a hard finish. Thank God, write one lesson, and plan a tiny upgrade.

91

GOD'S PLAN > MY SCHEDULE

"For I know the plans I have for you," declares the Lord, "plans to give you hope and a future." Jeremiah 29:11

Scout team helmet. Long meetings. Little spotlight. Brock Purdy kept stacking quiet days like bricks. He studied while others joked, prayed while others scrolled, and treated every rep like it mattered. Then a door opened. People called it sudden. Heaven called it right on time. Brock's peace came from months of trusting God's plan more than his own calendar. Jeremiah 29:11 is not a magic button. It is a warm promise in cold seasons. You might feel benched by life. Not starting. Overlooked. Give God your preparation. Show up early. Ask good questions. Cheer loud from the sideline. Pray, Guide my path, and watch how waiting turns into training. When opportunity knocks, you will not explode with panic. You will breathe and walk through with a ready heart. And if it takes longer, you are still winning, because trust roots deep where rush cannot grow.

Prayer:

Father, I surrender my timeline. Guide my path. Help me work with joy, serve with love, and trust Your timing.

Practice:

Write today's plan. Give it to God. Do small tasks excellently and welcome interruptions as training.

92

INFLUENCE STARTS SMALL

"Whoever can be trusted with very little can also be trusted with much."
Luke 16:10

The night the world held its breath for Damar Hamlin, prayers rose like fireworks. But years before that, influence grew in tiny rooms. He learned trainers' names. He fist bumped equipment staff. He checked on rookies who looked lost in oversized jerseys. Those little choices stacked into a life people trusted. Luke 16:10 says big doors swing on small hinges. Your hallway is full of hinges. Pick up tape scraps near the bench. Say good morning to the janitor. Share your snack with a freshman who forgot lunch. Whisper, Make me light, and watch what God does. Influence is not a blue check. It is a steady shine. When real moments arrive, you will not need to change. The spotlight will simply show who you already are. That is how light spreads in schools, teams, and cities, one quiet, faithful spark at a time.

Prayer:

Lord, make me a light in small places. Help me notice needs, act kindly, and lift people toward You.

Practice:

Encourage one person today. Speak life, then follow up with a simple helpful action.

93
WORK IS WORSHIP

"Whatever you do, whether in word or deed, do it all in the name of the Lord Jesus." Colossians 3:17

Tile after tile, Michael Phelps watches the pool floor scroll like a slow movie. Arms burn. Air feels thin. The clock keeps clicking its stubborn rhythm. Somewhere between the ache and the turn, he finds a groove that feels almost holy. Rhythm. Breath. Reach. Colossians 3:17 says every deed can sing God's name. That means your hardest drill can become a prayer. When your legs quiver, inhale and whisper, Be glorified. Offer the next rep like a gift. You stop performing for approval and start practicing for Presence. The pool becomes a chapel. The track becomes an altar. Teammates feel your calm. Coaches trust your steady. You start enjoying small improvements because each one is a thank you to the Giver. Work becomes worship, and worship adds meaning to the grind until ordinary effort glows.

Prayer:

God, take my work today. Be glorified in my words, attitude, focus, and sweat. Turn drills into worship.

Practice:

In the hardest drill, pause one breath. Pray Be glorified, then attack the rep with focus.

94

PURPOSE IN PRACTICE

"Commit to the Lord whatever you do, and he will establish your plans."
Proverbs 16:3

Empty gym hums like a seashell. LeBron James moves through details most people skip. Foot angle. Hip turn. Eye level on a kickout pass. He treats practice like a lab where excellence is built one careful test at a time. Proverbs 16:3 invites you into the same magic. Commit your practice to God and every rep gains meaning. Pick one drill and name it. Ball security. First step. Calm breath. Pray, Bless my reps, then track the work. A tally mark. A timer. A sticky note on your bottle. Celebrate tiny progress. Games slow down because your brain already solved the puzzle at half speed. Confidence rises because commitment gives roots. God does not ask for flawless. He asks for faithful. Offer your effort and watch Him establish something steady inside you that pressure cannot crack.

Prayer:

Lord, I commit my practice to You. Bless my reps. Shape my habits, sharpen my mind, and grow my love to compete.

Practice:

Choose one drill. Set a small target. Pray Bless my reps. Execute with focus and joy.

95

GIVE GOD THE GLORY

"If anyone serves, they should do so with the strength God provides, so that in all things God may be praised." 1 Peter 4:11

Arrow routes, cross body darts, cameras everywhere. Patrick Mahomes grins, points up, and thanks the big guys who guard him. That gesture is a tether that keeps his heart from floating away. First Peter 4:11 says our strength comes from God so the praise returns to God. When you hand glory back, you do not shrink. You shine in the right direction. After wins, gratitude keeps your feet on the ground. After losses, it keeps your hope alive. Try it in your world. In the locker room, thank the trainer who tapes ankles. Online, tag a verse with your highlight. Whisper, Keep me humble, before the mic finds you. People will feel peace around you, not just power, because your confidence is borrowed from a limitless Source.

Prayer:

Father, every skill is Your gift. Keep me humble. Let my words and work point hearts to Your goodness today.

Practice:

After your game, post thanks with a verse. Credit teammates, coaches, and God by name.

96
FAITH AFTER FAME

"Forgetting what is behind and straining toward what is ahead, I press on toward the goal." Philippians 3:13-14

Confetti falls like bright snow. Nick Foles hugs teammates while a city sings. Then the parade ends and the room gets quiet. New teams. New roles. New questions. He learns that faith cannot live in yesterday's trophy case. Paul writes about forgetting and pressing. That is not amnesia. It is direction. Celebrate, then move. Learn, then step. Nick chooses to refocus. He journals new goals, prays with teammates, and roots his identity in Christ, not in headlines. You will taste both fireworks and silence. Neither moment defines you. Jesus does. When your heart clings to the past or freezes in regret, pray, Refocus me. Ask for one brave step that builds character today. God loves to meet you in fresh starts. That is where joy returns, not as a shout from a crowd, but as a steady drum in your chest.

Prayer:

Jesus, thank You for past blessings. Refocus me now. Give me clear next steps, steady courage, and humble joy.

Practice:

Journal one fresh goal with God. Make it specific, team centered, and measurable.

97

ETERNAL SCOREBOARD

"Store up for yourselves treasures in heaven, where moth and rust do not destroy." Matthew 6:19-20

Loud week. Brighter lights. Jeremy Lin smiles as the world roars. Then the noise fades and minutes shrink. He learns a secret that saves his joy. There is another scoreboard. Heaven's points are people loved, prayers whispered, truth shared, generosity given. That board never glitches. Matthew 6 moves our eyes from trophies that dust will eat to treasures that last forever. Your stats matter, but they are not everything. Before you chase a medal, whisper, Value eternity. Encourage a teammate who rides the bench. Thank the team manager who washes jerseys. Give away the extra gear. Play free because your worth is fixed. When your heart plays for forever, you bring peace to today. Pressure loosens. Purpose grows. Wins turn into worship, and losses turn into lessons that still count as treasure.

Prayer:

Lord, fix my eyes on what lasts. Teach me to value people over prizes and love over likes today.

Practice:

Before any trophy moment, thank God. Then quietly encourage someone behind the scenes.

98

STAY FAITHFUL SMALL

"Well done, my good servant… because you have been trustworthy in a very small matter." Luke 19:17

Dawn paints the field pink. Mia Hamm taps the ball against a wall until the rhythm sounds like music. No crowd. Just shoes on grass and a heartbeat counting reps. Her greatness grew in tiny rooms. Stretch before sleep. Sprint through the line. Jog back on defense. Luke 19:17 says God celebrates small trust. Your future is built from daily bricks. Choose one good habit and guard it. Drink water first. Ten minutes of touches. Thank a coach after practice. Whisper, Help me steady, when you feel lazy. Small faithfulness becomes big trust. Coaches notice. Teammates copy. Confidence grows because your private choices match your public goals. When you are tempted to skip the little thing, remember that God sees and smiles. Keep laying bricks. Castles rise that way.

Prayer:

God, help me love small consistency. Strengthen my focus. Anchor my habits. Make my private work honor You.

Practice:

Pick one habit. Repeat it today. Track it. Protect it. Thank God for the strength to continue.

99

LEGACY OF LOVE

"Now these three remain: faith, hope and love. But the greatest of these is love." 1 Corinthians 13:13

Reggie White thundered off the edge like a storm, then prayed with the lineman he just sacked. He bought groceries for families, hugged kids, and spoke life into locker rooms. Love was his loudest stat. Paul says love is the greatest because people outlast seasons. You can start that legacy now. Sit with the quiet kid at lunch. Share gear. Defend a classmate with truth. Compete hard without cheap shots. Pray, Grow my love, and watch how God widens your heart. Love changes the temperature of a team. Practices feel safer. Games feel cleaner. Years from now, when numbers fade from memory, people will remember your kindness like a warm coat on a cold day. That is a legacy worth leaving.

Prayer:

Jesus, grow love in me. Make me patient, brave, and kind. Help me compete hard while honoring people.

Practice:

Do one hidden act of service. Carry bags, share water, or write a kind note.

100
PURPOSE BEYOND SPORT

"In all things God works for the good of those who love him." Romans 8:28

Locker room quiet. Cleats unstrapped. Season over. Julie Ertz learned that God's purpose keeps breathing after whistles stop. World Cups brought cheers, but family, service, and faith brought deeper joy. Romans 8:28 is a promise that God weaves good even through detours. Injury, graduation, position changes cannot cancel His plan. Ask Him how to love beyond your scoreboard. Tutor a classmate. Volunteer with younger players. Lead warmups with joy when you cannot play. Pray, Guide my next, and watch new doors open that fit your gifts. When identity leans only on sport, every setback feels like a collapse. When identity rests in Jesus, new chapters feel like adventure. Your life becomes a bigger field where love runs farther than any sprint.

Prayer:

Father, thank You for my sport and my future. Guide my next steps. Use me to serve and shine Your love.

Practice:

Give thirty minutes to help. Tutor, volunteer, or clean a space at school with joy.

101
FINISH THE RACE

"I have fought the good fight, I have finished the race, I have kept the faith." (2 Timothy 4:7)

Tyson Fury, heavyweight boxer, knows some battles happen outside the ring. Injuries, headlines, heavy thoughts. On a quiet night he jogs under streetlights, shoes tapping a steady beat. He remembers Paul's words to Timothy. Life is not one explosive round. It is a long race. Some miles glide. Some miles feel like mud. The goal is not just a belt. The goal is finishing with faith. He sets checkpoints he can keep. Call a friend. Stretch. Pray. Sleep. Repeat. Small finishes build big finishers. In your season, finishing looks like turning work in on time, showing up for teammates, and getting up when you fall. Celebrate wins, then keep moving. If you stumble, confess fast and restart.

Pray, Let me finish well. God cares how you cross the line, not only how you blast from the blocks. Endurance grows one honest lap at a time. Look forward, breathe steady, trust Jesus, and take the next step with courage each day. Champions, famous and unseen, share the same rhythm. They show up, give honest effort, and trust God with the clock.

Prayer:

Lord, give me endurance and humility. When I'm weary, lift me. Help me keep the faith and finish well. Amen.

Practice:

Review your week. Keep one strong habit. Replace one weak habit. Start fresh tomorrow morning.

CONCLUSION: KEEP GOING

The gym is quiet again.

Sweat still shines on the floor.

Your heartbeat is slowing down, but your spirit feels wide awake.

You made it. You finished every story, every verse, every challenge that asked you to grow stronger inside and out. That is something to celebrate. You kept showing up. You learned how to stay calm when pressure hit. You built habits that will follow you into every part of life.

You prayed before you scrolled. You practiced when no one watched. You found peace when everyone else felt panic. You learned to see training as worship and to play for something bigger than applause. That is real championship living.

You are now part of a small group of people who understand what it means to keep faith in the middle of the grind. Steph Curry does it before sunrise. Simone Biles does it when the world is watching. Giannis does it in extra drills that no one counts. You are doing it too, one choice at a time.

Champions are not perfect. They just keep returning. They take what they learn and use it again tomorrow. When you mess up or miss a day, you do not lose your progress. You gain another chance to restart. That is what growth looks like. That is what faith feels like.

When you walk out of this book, do not leave the lessons behind. Bring them into the classroom, the locker room, the field, and the hallways. Remember that God trains you in every space, not just in prayer time. The same peace that steadied you during these readings can show up when the crowd is loud or when a test feels impossible.

If you ever feel stuck, come back to a page that spoke to you. Reread it. Whisper the prayer again. The same God who met you here is still listening.

He never stops coaching. He never stops believing in you.

And this is not the end. This is your start.

You have built a foundation that will keep growing. You have learned to trust, to focus, and to breathe when things get hard. There is so much more ahead.

I have more for you too. More stories. More devotionals. More ways to grow your game and your faith at the same time. Keep your eyes open for what is coming next. There are new challenges, new verses, and new plays to add to your spiritual training plan.

Until then, stay ready. Keep praying first. Keep showing up early. Keep finishing strong.

Your life is the arena now. Your mindset is your gear. Your faith is your superpower.

God called you to be a champion.

You already are one.

Now go live like it

A QUICK BLESSING

Your feedback is a true blessing!

If this book has encouraged you or helped you feel less alone, would you leave a quick review?

Even one sentence makes a huge difference and takes just a minute. As a small author, your feedback not only lifts my heart... it also helps other women of faith with find the support and hope they need.

Thank you for being part of this journey!

Scan this QR code with your phone to go to the review page

Or

Go to your orders, find the book and click

"Write a product review"

Thank you <3

If you liked this book, you can check out our other books as well:

Scan the QR to see my books on my author page!

Like this one: Called to be a Champion for Girls

www.ingramcontent.com/pod-product-compliance
Lightning Source LLC
Chambersburg PA
CBHW071520120626
46550CB00006B/2290